COLLAPSE FEMINISM

COLLAPSE FEMINISM

The Online Battle for Feminism's Future

Alice Cappelle

Published by Repeater Books

An imprint of Watkins Media Ltd

Unit 11 Shepperton House

89-93 Shepperton Road

London

N1 3DF

United Kingdom

www.repeaterbooks.com

A Repeater Books paperback original 2023

1

Distributed in the United States by Random House, Inc., New York.

Copyright Alice Cappelle © 2023

Alice Cappelle asserts the moral right to be identified as the author of this work.

ISBN: 9781915672018

Ebook ISBN: 9781915672292

Printed and bound in the United Kingdom by TJ Books Limited

Contents

A practical scheme, says Oscar Wilde, is either one already in existence, or a scheme that could be carried out under the existing conditions; but it is exactly the existing conditions that one objects to, and any scheme that could accept these conditions is wrong and foolish.

— Emma Goldman, 1910

Preface

We're doomed.

We hear this phrase more and more frequently. The ultra-wealthy are already building bunkers in their gardens and space rockets to escape the Earth, groups of young people — called "doomers" — have given up the fight, and fascism is on the rise across Europe. The fatalistic idea that civilisation is quickly approaching collapse has become the framework through which we write, debate, theorise and therefore make society. Such a framework provides fertile ground for the development of conservative ideas in mainstream discourse, since, in times of fear, people are more likely to turn in on themselves and look backwards for answers. Unsurprisingly, the narrative of collapse, replacement, or destitution — that is too often pushed by the powerful — doesn't foster social action.

What happens to feminism in this context? Nothing good, really, and that is precisely why I'm writing this book. Amnesty International has warned of a dramatic deterioration of women's rights worldwide.[1] In France, the country I was born and live in, the *Haut Conseil à l'Égalité entre les femmes et les hommes* (High Council for Equality between Women and Men) established sexism barometers and discovered that sexism is "stagnating" and "advancing" in some areas.[2] In the US, writer Samhita Mukhopadhyay was surprised to see so few women protesting the overturn of the *Roe v. Wade* decision when compared to the Black Lives Matter protests or the Women's March.[3] "There's more raw misogyny now", says feminist author Susan Faludi in a *New York Times* article titled "The Future Isn't Female Anymore".[4]

Why "collapse feminism"? Collapse feminism considers the predominance of the narrative of collapse but turns it upside down. It seeks inspiration from people at the margins who refuse to settle for fatalism precisely because their existence depends on believing that things can get better.

As a white, Western woman, I started writing this book with the intention for it to have the broadest possible appeal. When people enthusiastically asked me what I was writing about, I struggled to say the word "feminism" because of its negative connotations. When asked what they think about feminism, most men reply they agree with gender equality, but that the movement has gone too far, it has become too extreme.[5] This is not surprising, given that very little media space is left for feminist activists and thinkers to explain what the movement stands for. The misconceptions around what feminism is can also be related to the multitude of feminisms that now exist. I do not have the authority — no one has — to decide what feminism is and what it isn't. However, I can say that feminism to me is bigger than gender equality, it's bigger than women; it's a social project, a vision of how things could be if we ditched the culture of domination that the patriarchy nurtures. In a patriarchal world, people take, use and throw away. In a feminist world, people would prioritise care. *It's a bold claim*, some will say, *but it sounds a bit naive*. It is true that I probably wouldn't have written that when I started thinking about what I wanted to do with this book. However, as I searched for progressive alternatives to the conservative ideas I'll be criticising in this book, I was almost systematically redirected to feminist literature, in all its diversity. I concluded that intersectional feminism offered some of the best answers to the challenges of our time. Sure, feminism won't come up with a protocol on how to decarbonise our economies. It is not a program, an authoritative force, but an *invitation* to boldly rethink the basis upon which we make society.

When I talked about my book to left-wing men, a complaint I often heard was: "What about class?" There are many different lenses through which one can approach the ills of society, and class struggle is one of them, but I chose gender instead, and I'll explain why. Historically, social justice movements like feminism, anti-racism, LGBTQ+ movements, etc., have had to negotiate with dominant left-wing parties to be part of their class-centred agenda.[6] As effective grassroots movements that converted the support they received into left-wing votes, the level of recognition given to them by left-wing party leaders has rarely been fair. Western feminists have often pointed out the hypocrisy of left-wing leaders who were feminist only for the duration of their campaigns. I, as well as other leftist women and a significant number of leftist men, were extremely disappointed by Jean-Luc Mélenchon, the president of the 2022 French left-wing coalition, when he fervently defended a party leader accused of domestic violence.[7] The female party members who criticised him were immediately accused of hurting the movement. But women, and minority groups in general, are fed up with having to shut up for "the benefit of the cause". How are we supposed to support a movement that betrays us? If a left-wing revolution is to happen, then there is a lot of foundational work to be done. That is precisely what the feminist project is all about: abolishing the culture of domination in all aspects of society to forge instead a *collective of differences*. It's a radical project, but to paraphrase and expand on anarchist feminist Emma Goldman's words, if women and marginalised folks "can't dance to it, it won't be [our] revolution!"[8]

I grounded this work in internet culture because I believe in its potential for experimentation. In a way, this book can also serve as an introduction to the online world, which is weirdly fascinating. The internet, and more specifically social media, have become *the* place where people of different generations seek entertainment, information, and forge their opinions. Understanding how it functions has become a prerogative of contemporary political movements. The internet can be our best friend or our worst enemy. It connects people sharing similar interests and values but can also foster dangerous echo chambers when not used carefully. Even if it is currently dominated by Big Tech, the internet — from submarine cables to the computer screen, or from Wikipedia articles to that bad review you posted on Google last week — is made by the people.[9] It is a space for peer-to-peer collaboration, as well as social, political and artistic experimentation. However, like any other institution, it mirrors everything that is wrong with how we make society. The internet both reflects and influences people's beliefs. In particular, this book looks at how conservatives utilise the internet to disseminate their ideas in political as well as apolitical communities.

The first part explores how women online are drawn to a specific ideal of womanhood. The first chapter looks at the successive downfalls of all types of girlbosses, from the "Lean In" feminist to *that girl*, and at the reconsideration of work as synonymous with liberation. The second chapter dives deep into female online communities that promote a return to traditional living. Presented as a form of liberation from the constraints of neoliberal hustle culture, traditional living is said to preserve a woman's agency because it is motivated by the feminist act of choosing for oneself.

The second part aims at drawing attention to the implications of the now common assertion that the sexual revolution was a failure. In fact, the criticism of some of the by-products of sexual liberation — including hook-up culture and dating apps — serves as the foundation of a larger critique of the deregulation of female sexuality, targeted as the root of all societal ills. The first chapter starts by describing the reactionary backlash against women powered by men, who — to twist feminist scholar bell hooks' words — *do not* have the will to change. It then proceeds to broaden the scope of analysis to include liberal, left-wing and even feminist critiques of the sexual revolution. Finally, the second chapter strengthens the argument that the systematic attacks on female sexual liberation foster the belief in the need for a return to a conservative, pure and family-oriented society.

My goal isn't merely to critique or point a finger at a constructed enemy. "Critique is essential to doing the work of clarifying the nature of trouble", said feminist scholar Donna Haraway, "the problem [...] is stopping with critique. And nothing but critique."[10] The legacy of feminism is a collection of bold and innovative alternatives forged by women across communities and territories to fight back against the patriarchal domination over living beings. It would be a shame not to honour that in a book that, surely, sounds alarming, but wants to remain hopeful. Despite the attacks it faces and the enthusiastic proclamations of its death, the feminist movement is alive and kicking. It is ambitious, all-encompassing, and I hope this book will convince you to further engage with what it has to say, if not fully embrace it.

Part I: The Ideal Woman

Seven years ago, I stumbled upon a YouTube video titled "Women's Ideal Body Types Throughout History". The video, published by *BuzzFeed*, has now more than fifty million views. As the title indicates, ideal body types from Ancient Egypt to modern day, from the slender body and symmetrical facial features of Egyptian queens to Kim Kardashian's slim-thick silhouette, are successively presented to the viewer. The features of each body type are highlighted, implying that one must have them all to earn the label of ideal body type. At least that is what my seventeen-year-old self thought when she watched the video for the first time, eagerly looking for features she already had, feeling validated with every box ticked. It is not surprising that *BuzzFeed* commissioned the video. With all its personality quizzes and pop culture media coverage, the platform has capitalised on young people's never-ending quest for a stable sense of identity. On social media, users like to fit into specific aesthetics like "that girl", "e-girl", "grunge", "tradwife", "cottagecore", "dark academia", "y2k", "minimalism". These are built around a list of products to own and a set of personality traits and behaviours to perform. *BuzzFeed* and social media not only promote "aesthetics", but also serve as platforms where users turn them into subcultures and online communities.

At the heart of the appeal of aesthetics is what psychoanalyst Jacques Lacan called the *Ideal-I*, a "fantasy image of oneself

[that] can be filled in by others who we may want to emulate in our adult lives (role models, etc.), anyone that we set up as a mirror for ourselves".[1] Commenting on Lacan's findings, Jonah Peretti, the founder of *BuzzFeed* — who used to write anti-capitalist essays — added that "the increasingly rapid rate at which images are distributed and consumed in late capitalism necessitates a corresponding increase in the rate that individuals assume and shed identities".[2] Individuals switching from one aesthetic to another, aiming for their *Ideal-I,* have what he calls "weak egos". The advertisement industry heavily relies on those weak egos for the sale of products, clothes and home decor. New me equals new aesthetic, new hair, new clothes, new vibe. It is not surprising that closet decluttering videos, as well as fashion and homeware hauls, attract so many viewers. They materialise the never-ending cycle of self-formation from the rejection of the past self to the "new me", all sponsored by capitalism.

The acceleration of the process of the creation and dissolution of the self is coherent with larger cultural trends happening at a local and global scale. Starting in the nineteenth century, the industrial revolution triggered the displacement of people from the countryside to the city, but also from non-industrialised countries to Western economic powers. As twentieth-century literary classics like Theodore Dreiser's *Sister Carrie* or Richard Wright's *Black Boy* describe, the city was seen as a locus for the formation of a new self, detached from familial and religious traditions and conservative ideologies. Using contemporary social media terminology, we could say that eighteen-year-old Sister Carrie and nineteen-year-old Richard Wright had "main character energy".

This phrase became popular as stories of people who moved to big cities like New York, London and Paris gained traction online. Generally speaking, "moving" vlogs perform very well when compared to other kinds of lifestyle content precisely because they signal renewal and change. People who get a chance to become those main characters are often freelancers, artists and highly skilled workers. This complex group of individuals, reduced by some to the "creative class",[3] gave rise to its own aesthetic, the hipster aesthetic, which, in internet years, belongs to a former geological era. Like other popular online aesthetics, the hipster aesthetic gathered several of its own key attributes, including the flannel shirt, the moustache print, the beanie, stripes, denim, edgy colours, etc. However, the hipster was soon mocked for embodying something bigger than a mere aesthetic. Being a hipster became synonymous with being a gentrifier, and that is not something anyone would want to brag about. In fact, the aesthetic was understood as more than cosplay (a costume and lifestyle one choses to adopt as self-expression), it had social implications.

Since the hipster's (semi-) downfall, many aesthetics have appeared, disappeared and reappeared, but one feature remains unchanged: an aesthetic continues to be understood as more than cosplay. In some cases, it's an invitation to a different worldview; in others, it serves to spot and frame the enemy. As the symbol of the "liberal creative gentrifier", the hipster quickly became the enemy of pretty much everybody except hipsters. In today's on- and offline discourses, aesthetics embody a cultural moment, they are a statement in and of itself with which people can agree or disagree. This first part of this section looks specifically at how the aesthetic of womanhood is regulated online. But before we do that, it is necessary to grasp the structure and functioning of online politics.

Perceived as a form of speech, aesthetics are used by political groups to facilitate communication. For example, on social media, in the process of arguing against a left-wing man, a right-wing person might call them a "soyboy". The term soyboy used to refer to men who were deemed weak and effeminate, but is now used to target any left-leaning man who is an ally to oppressed groups. In another example, in late October 2022, UK Home Secretary and Conservative MP Suella Braverman blamed the "*Guardian*-reading, tofu-eating wokeratis"[4] for eco-protests. Alongside the right's obsession with tofu and soyboys, "the blue hair feminist" and the androgynous "social justice warrior" are also often mobilised. They become signs to which a series of concepts are attached — identity politics, snowflake, political correctness and cancel culture, to name a few. The "soyboy", the "blue hair feminist", and the "social justice warrior" are stereotypes of what is defined as the online left. This represents a section of the left-wing electorate which has forged its political identity on social media, values intersectionality and social and climate justice, and which often practises scepticism to the point of nihilism. Obviously, reducing the diversity of left-wing online users to one definition is fl\awed. In reaction to the caricatural depictions of the online left, some leftists — almost exclusively young white men — have distanced themselves from identity politics in a "not like the other leftists" manner, instead claiming that they want to "go back to the essential", meaning to revive the universalism of class struggle politics in opposition to identity politics. In doing so, they participate in what is now commonly referred to as the "culture wars".

The phrase "cultural war"[5] was first used by right-wing political commentator Pat Buchanan during the 1992 Republican National Convention to describe what was at stake in the upcoming election between Democrat Bill Clinton and Republican George Bush. Buchanan saw Bill Clinton's pro-gay-rights agenda, his wife's "radical feminism" (yes, he was referring to Hillary Clinton), and Vice President Al Gore's environmentalism as a threat to American culture. Flashforward to today, where the culture wars are a regular topic of discussion on right-wing online platforms and TV shows. They materialise two easily identifiable groups, each gathered around a set of values: orthodoxy, tradition and normativity on one side; and progressivism, critique and reform on the other.[6] The first group is identified as conservatives, while the other group is made of progressives (often caricatured as "woke").

The existence of a phrase like "culture wars" reflects a societal malaise, a refusal to recognise that gender, sex, race, or more concretely memorial statues and history books, are not disconnected from politics. They are in fact deeply political. On TV, reactionary political commentators like Tucker Carlson in the US or Piers Morgan in the UK have turned the culture wars into a profitable business. Gathering millions of viewers, they denounce the destruction of what made our societies great by the "woke industrial complex"[7], "woke incorporated"[8] and "the Cathedral".[9] All these terms point at the influence academia has on liberal journalism, Big Tech, and society in general. Identity politics are woke people's weapon, they say. Those social justice warrior snowflakes see racism, sexism and homophobia everywhere, in every one of us. In fact, now that minorities have started to have a voice and are demanding that we consider their specificity, those who have benefited from silencing them are quick to reverse the victim/oppressor paradigm. Sure, the feeling of loss and fear is a natural reaction to societal change. One way to approach that feeling is to understand its roots, to question its legitimacy, to "deconstruct" it. However, another way to approach it consists of adopting a reactionary stance, to let it grow, and politicise it into an identity crisis.

The Conservative Online Ecosystem

Now that we have looked at the role that images and aesthetics play in the online "culture wars", it is time to zoom into its conservative component. First and foremost, it must be pointed out that while social media are very Western-centric — US-centric, to be specific — they reach users from all over the world. When I talk about US politics or culture in my YouTube videos, I regularly receive comments from North Americans who ask me to stay away from their country's affairs and mind my own business. They fail to understand that the North American conservative ecosystem is a source of inspiration for conservatives in other countries. In France, *par exemple*, the discourse of the supporters of far-right politicians Marine Le Pen and Éric Zemmour is very similar to that of US conservative megastar Ben Shapiro. In fact, translated videos of Shapiro and other conservative influencers perform very well on French YouTube, and controversial figures like Steven Crowder and Andrew Tate are replaced by, let's say, Julien Rochedy and Papacito.

The second defining feature of the conservative online ecosystem is that it has understood the potential of outrage to foster engagement (views, likes and comments). Outrage refers to both the form and content. The content is outrageous in the sense that it is *purposely* not politically correct. It aims to trigger sensibilities, as Shapiro's infamous phrase "facts don't care about your feelings" indicates. The online right navigates platforms' guidelines with the confidence of always coming out on top. On the one hand, they use a dog whistle, a coded language meant to convey a message to a specific audience without appearing too problematic. As an example, conservatives have often campaigned for the "protection of children" as a way to oppose LGBT communities' fight for their rights. This dog whistle allows them to share their political message to the masses and comply with social media's strict anti-hate speech guidelines. That way, they avoid bans and demonetisation, meaning the removal of ads on their content which leads to a decrease in revenue. On the other hand, they occasionally use hate speech to seek demonetisation and bans for the purpose of denouncing Big Tech as an Orwellian anti-free speech police.

In terms of form, outrage is materialised through titles and video thumbnails that are produced in a way that dramatises the issue at stake. Portions of the title appear in capital letters, punctuation is exaggerated, the terms "owned", "destroyed", "ripped" and "humiliated" are common. This pattern mimics toxic debate culture as it creates an environment where the online left and right are teams constantly fighting each other, proving the other side is wrong and morally bad.

Debate culture has also been appropriated by several leftists who feel it is necessary to engage in it to counter the right's online influence. They use a similar "outrage" aesthetic and seek to beat the right at its own game. It is certain that some of that content has been effective at denouncing misogynistic influencers like Andrew Tate and has provided a necessary debunking of the ideology of conservative thinkers like Jordan B. Peterson. Unfortunately, it also amplifies a debate culture that ultimately benefits the right. Despite their complaints of censorship and attacks on free speech, the online right currently dominates social media platforms in terms of presence, views and engagement. On top of having the financial support of structures like *The Daily Wire*, *Prager U* and private donors, they can also rely on an army of fans who turn every piece of content they produce into YouTube shorts, TikTok videos, Instagram reels, and so on, so that conservative ideas spread across the internet.

Conservative men make up the biggest chunk of the ecosystem. Ben Shapiro was already mentioned as one of the leading figures of the online conservative ecosystem. He co-founded *The Daily Wire*, which is one of the most influential conservative media structures. Relying on a capitalist business model that adapts to the demands of the online world, *The Daily Wire* is different from another big conservative non-profit institution, *Prager U*. The name "Prager University" was inspired by one of its founders, Dennis Prager, a conservative radio talk host who has often been at war with YouTube because of serious disinformation cases.[10] Nevertheless, the *Prager U* YouTube channel has attracted millions of subscribers and more than a billion and a half views since its creation in 2009. Focusing on short, animated, educational content, the channel seeks to provide a conservative point of view on history, education, politics and so on. Both *The Daily Wire* and *Prager U* are very open about their political agenda. They both invest or plan on investing into kids' content to counter what they call "gender ideology"[11] and allow their hosts and guests to be open about their religious beliefs and ideological upbringing.

In mid-2022, *Daily Wire+*, a subscription streaming program connected to *The Daily Wire* welcomed a new member to its team: Jordan B. Peterson. The collaboration was the final step to connect all parts of the online conservative ecosystem. Jordan B. Peterson is an incredibly popular figure, with more than 3.5 million followers on Twitter and 5.9 million subscribers on YouTube. Through self-help and theological educational content, Peterson managed to gain popularity primarily among young men seeking life guidance. His work as an academic and self-help guru are, according to video essayist Natalie Wynn, "a Trojan horse for a reactionary political agenda".[12]

One theme regularly explored by the male conservative ecosystem relevant to this book is that of "the crisis of masculinity". It is loosely defined by its proponents as men's struggle to adjust and develop their masculinity in a society that seeks to change its meaning. Some men see that change as necessary. The challenges that come with it are envisioned as an opportunity to become better human beings. For other (somehow very loud) men, such a change imposed by feminism is unnatural and will lead to society's downfall. The recent re-emergence of "the crisis of masculinity" in public discourse is largely in response to the #MeToo movement. It is the psychological component of the anti-feminist backlash. However, the researcher Francis Dupuis-Déri has shown there isn't anything new about the crisis of masculinity. A quick search on the internet made him realise that it already existed in Ancient Rome, in the English and French kingdoms at the end of the Middle Ages, again in England in the eighteenth century, during the French revolution, in Germany at the beginning of the nineteenth century and towards the end of the twentieth century, in France, the US and British colonies towards the end of the nineteenth century and beginning of the twentieth, between the two World Wars, in the 1950s and 1960s in the US, Germany and USSR, and has spread since the 1990s in the West, in Maghreb, Morocco, Ivory Coast, Senegal, Kenya, Tanzania, Darfur, in Latin America, and also in Japan, China, Bangladesh, Mongolia, Palestine, Iran and Israel.[13]

So, are men interminably in crisis?[14] There is a big discrepancy between men's feelings of emasculation and the relative power they hold in society, in both the public and private spheres. So why does this rhetoric work so well? The answer provided by right-wing media is that men relate to it, and you can't take that away from them, you can't dictate how they should feel about their existence in the world. Sure, but facts don't care about your feelings, I'd dare to say. No problem, answers Professor Richard V. Reeves, author of *Of Boys and Men*, which has the goal of shedding light on the modern man's struggle in school, at work and in the family.

Of Boys and Men was acclaimed by right-wing and liberal critics; finally, someone was talking about the downfall of men. It starts with the premise that we live in a post-feminist world. The author then proceeds to argue that a new form of gender inequality is emerging as women are outperforming men in various branches of society, including school and university. While it is true that men are underperforming in several areas, does that mean men as a sex-class are in crisis? Reeves doesn't belong to the conservative ecosystem, he's a liberal, but his stance very much aligns with conservatives' strategy to pathologize social evolutions that benefit women into a masculinity crisis. As a researcher, Reeves could have analysed the disparities he recorded through different frameworks. The fact that he chose *gender* means that, to him, it is because of their gender that men are underperforming in certain areas. That is the perspective he wanted to prioritise, but this choice has consequences. In fact, it is coherent with a discourse that has emerged in the "manosphere", a network of online men's communities that are characterised by anti-feminist and sexist beliefs. They argue that men are facing discrimination in society and in their lives on the basis that they are men. Such a discourse extends to the point of asserting that women are on the path of taking control over society. So, let's be clear. Men continue to hold a significant amount of social, economic and political power, even in the areas where women outperform them in numbers. There is no matriarchy and no plans to create one.

Men's rights activists, and by extension the manosphere, don't care about liberal nuance and disclaimers. They will take anything that helps them strengthen their own agenda, and having a respectable liberal like Reeves go in their direction is more than they could ever ask for. At a time when the manosphere is growing, when feminism is being attacked from every corner, Reeves' choice to make of male gender inequality something one can think and theorise is concerning, as it gives people yet another reason to blame it all on women. As we will see throughout this book, the liberal tendency to consider reactionary points of view as a legitimate basis from which to think or debate is responsible for the standardisation of those very points of views.

On social media, the crisis of masculinity translates into the attention and sympathy we give to "lonely, single men" and the growing aversion for "picky women". Heterosexual men are described as disoriented, unable to date or to form relationships with women. In the "post-feminist" world we live in, lonely men have become "the marginalised".[15] The impact of loneliness on both young men and women is undeniably severe. However, the way it is often reduced to a men's issue and then instrumentalised to anti-feminist ends is alarming. It is precisely through the crisis of masculinity rhetoric that the conservative online ecosystem draws an increasing number of young men to its cause. Once those are set on the right algorithmic track, it doesn't take long for them to be politically radicalised.

The woman's side of the online conservative ecosystem is less homogenous. Women are divided into two connected groups: the lifestyle sphere and the political sphere. Let's concentrate here on the political sphere, as we will analyse the lifestyle sphere in Chapter 2. Social and political commentators Candace Owens, Mikhaila Peterson and Brett Cooper are the most influential people in that sphere. Some of these women describe themselves as conservative, others as libertarian, sometimes both. In their sphere, they are simultaneously perceived as the spokesperson of conservative women and outside the category of "women". Their role is to reinforce conservative men's talking points to the point of appearing just as misogynistic as them. When invited on *The Full Send Podcast*, Candace Owens kept repeating to the young male hosts how much she hated modern-day feminism because it refused to acknowledge biological predispositions in men and women. She used the example of her school girlfriends who *naturally* went into communications and fashion as proof of that. She also added that women want to be married and have kids, that feminism has pushed women out of the kitchen and made them miserable.[16] Her complaints echo Elisabeth Elliot's 1976 popular manifesto *Let Me Be a Woman*, in which she explained that feminism has distorted what it means to be a woman, forcing women to adopt masculine criteria. She did not go as far as calling it a crisis of femininity, but I wouldn't be surprised if conservative women started using this phrase. *Let Me Be a Woman* implies that there is only one right way to be a woman, the *natural* way. Interestingly enough, Candace Owens simultaneously shares Elliot's opinions and contradicts them. Sure, she is married, she has kids, but she also has a very successful career outside the kitchen and people to whom she can transfer domestic responsibilities. She fails to be a credible representative of (conservative) women, a group she refers to using the pronouns "they/them" more than the pronouns "we/us". With their public influence and financial independence, Candace Owens, Brett Cooper and Mikhaila Peterson are exceptions to their own definition of what a woman is supposed to be.

In *Backlash*, journalist Susan Faludi mobilised a selection of interviews she conducted with leading anti-feminists of the 1980s. Among them was Beverly LaHaye, an American Christian conservative activist who founded Concerned Women for America in California, in 1979. Like Owens and Elliot, LaHaye claimed that a woman belongs to the domestic sphere, and that it is not in her nature to be ambitious.[17] However, Faludi didn't recognise LaHaye in that definition, for she remembered entering her Oval Office in which she saw a big flag planted next to the desk, pink curtains, business cards, and a picture of her shaking hands with Ronald Reagan. She learned that no one in the organisation was allowed to speak to LaHaye without her permission, but also that the conservative woman had just appointed herself president for life (typical girlboss behaviour).

When asked by a journalist what motivates LaHaye and what her philosophy is, Faludi answered that "what drives [LaHaye] is this human need to be engaged in the public world, to experience public life and to feel as if you are a part of it, and as if you're making some change".[18] Beverly LaHaye found a way to have her cake and eat it; to remain part of her conservative Christian community and gain influence as an individual by engaging in public life. Today's online conservative women follow in LaHaye's footsteps. They work on making it increasingly harder for women to be as fulfilled in their lives and careers as they are.

Now that all the terms have been defined, it is finally time to engage with the title of this part — The Ideal Woman — the cool, desirable, girlfriend material, or even marriageable woman. What do we expect from her? How do we want to forge her?

In the fight to gain respectability, the Black newspaper *The Colored Man* asserted in 1902 that a race cannot elevate itself above its women.[19] The degree of respectability of women is used as a mirror reflecting the well-being of the couple, family, or community unit, as well as society in its entirety. Women know it too well, they have been self-regulating themselves — their body, sexuality, looks, speech, occupations — for centuries to preserve each unit. In liberal societies, feminist movements have liberated women from many of the imperatives imposed on them. They have also broken down some of the material conditions that form the basis of their oppression. However, advances have systematically been met with a conservative backlash seeking to re-establish the "natural order of things". As mentioned previously, this first part aims to characterise the regulation of womanhood online by first looking at the downfall of all forms of girlboss content and, with it, the idea of work as liberation. It then examines how traditional living advocates use lifestyle content to become the new counterculture.

Chapter 1
What Happens When Work Is No Longer Synonymous with Liberation?

Girlboss ~~Fascism~~ Feminism

On September 23, 2022, *Politico Europe* tweeted:

> In 1992, a 15-year-old schoolgirl went to join her local branch of the far-right Youth Front in Rome. The all-male group of radicals met her with bemusement. Thirty years later, Giorgia Meloni is on course to become Italy's first female prime minister.[1]

Giorgia Meloni defines herself as "Italian, Christian, woman, mother", not "citizen x, gender x, parent 1, parent 2".[2] She wants to bring back conservative values as she believes her country is facing a culture war. Her party, *Fratelli d'Italia* (Brothers of Italy), is associated with neo-fascist groups that stretch back to Mussolini's era. At forty-five years old, the blue-eyed blonde is portrayed as a girlboss by mainstream media. In fact, *Politico Europe*'s tweet is a good example of how the girlboss filter magically cancels anything remotely problematic. Hillary Clinton herself greeted Meloni's potential win by saying that "every time a woman is elected to head of state or government, that is a step forward".[3] Representation matters, true. But Meloni's political agenda matters more, and it happens to oppose women's rights.

The "girlboss" in girlboss feminism comes from the title of entrepreneur Sophia Amoruso's 2014 best-selling book *#Girlboss*. Turned into a hashtag, the girlboss grew exponentially online as it got featured on posts, in videos, podcasts, and even inspired a Netflix TV series. Girlboss became synonymous with female empowerment in the workplace. It hoped to bridge representation gaps in leadership and managerial positions with pep talks and motivational quotes. Ultimately, the girlboss drew criticism for its marketing appeal and detachment from the reality of work. The issue at the core of girlboss feminism is that it overfocuses on individual empowerment without questioning how the individual got where they are, the nature of their power, and how they use it. For instance, Meloni strongly opposes "pink quotas" which help bridge representation gaps between men and women in all branches of the workforce.[4] On the contrary, she — like Thatcher and many other conservative girlbosses after her — value merit and assert that merit has no gender. Meloni bragged that her party was the only one that gathered several women in leadership positions. Similarly in France, Marine Le Pen's *Rassemblement National* (National Rally) counts an unusual number of gay men in leadership positions when compared to other political groups. However, the women and gay men of far-right parties do not politicise their identity. Their compliance with traditional values makes them safe and even benefits their political group, allowing them to appear less extreme, and therefore more electable.

While it may look inclusive, girlboss feminism perpetuates a culture of oppression. As bell hooks stated in *all about love*, "the rugged individual that can rely on no one else is a figure that can only exist in a culture of domination".[5] Capitalist feminists sought to prove that a woman can do anything a man does: lead, negotiate, command respect, earn a lot of money, and flex it all. Their message gained momentum with the release of former Facebook COO Sheryl Sandberg's *Lean In*, in which she explains that women are responsible for their lack of representation in leading positions. She theorised three rules for them to change that:

1) Sit at the table.
2) Make your partner a real partner.
3) Don't leave before you leave.

Rule number one is about forcing women to do what men already do: negotiate their entry salary, ask for promotions, literally sit at the table, ask questions, and own their success. Rule number two addresses the personal: working couples must become partners in raising their children, taking care of them so that women can find a better work-life balance. Finally, rule number three encourages women to not put their career on hold as soon as the prospect of building a family pops in their head. She tells them that such behaviour might lead them to miss a promotion that could be offered to a male colleague instead. After watching the corresponding TED Talk, I checked the comments section to see who was commenting and what the audience got from the video. As I'm writing, the top part of the comments section includes contributions from men and women who loved the talk. One male viewer said:

What I like specifically about this speech is that she isn't blaming men but pointing out how women subconsciously choose not to be assertive and points out how women should tell themselves to reach for the top, if they want to be on top. While men already are doing that.

This type of comment isn't surprising. Sandberg rolled out the red carpet for such takes. In fact, the constant comparison between men and women based on the premise that men do it right and women don't isn't nuanced by Sandberg at any point in her talk. An honest take on representation gaps would have, at least, included that the workplace is an environment that was historically designed by men for men. Some women do perform well in those structures because they have more assertive personalities, a characteristic most men are raised to adopt, and most women are raised to tone down. By refusing to address this reality, Sandberg's practical advice feels a bit humiliating. It supports the idea that women's value in the workplace depends on their ability to act like men. As seen in the comments section of the video, many men enjoyed her talk because it displaced their perceived guilt as embodiment of the patriarchy on women. Sandberg is different from feminists who seek to change the rules of the system or introduce affirmative action programs. She supports equality of opportunities and not equality of outcomes. If life was a race, equality of opportunities would mean that we all start on the same line regardless of our race, class, gender, health, etc., and the best of us would finish first. On the other hand, equality of outcome ditches the idea that life is a race and simply wants to ensure that all individuals, regardless of their specific identities, get to enjoy approximately the same conditions of life and levels of wealth. Sandberg understands that women must overcome more obstacles because of their gender but believes they should do so while starting on the same line as men. In the end, Sandberg embodies a form of moderate, individualist feminism that turns resentment towards gender inequality into judgement towards other women.[6]

Now don't get me wrong, I agree that at an individual level, women should be encouraged to ask for promotions, that they shouldn't feel like they can't sit at the table. However, it is necessary to detach ourselves from a purely individualistic approach and rethink the whole problem. First, while Sandberg is lucky enough to work in an environment where women are treated more or less equally to men, gender discrimination in the workplace is still very common. That reality is to be compounded with the potential biases of co-workers, clients and partners that can also have an impact on one's success at work. Sociologist Pierre Bourdieu coined the phrase "symbolic violence" in the 1970s to address this form of non-physical violence that allows power relations to reproduce themselves unchallenged. As an example, his book *Masculine Domination* investigates how language reflects unequal power relations between men and women. German sociologist Beate Krais expanded on Bourdieu's work to show that one could find symbolic violence in the way we portray female behaviours as weak: "to run like a girl", "to play like a girl".[7] Bourdieu stressed how symbolic violence isn't systematically deliberate and can therefore be reproduced by people who are themselves victims of that form of violence. The surrealist movie *Sorry To Bother You*, directed by Boots Riley, offers a good example of what symbolic violence looks like. The film follows Cassius Green, a young Black man struggling to make ends meet. He ends up getting a job as a telemarketer but can't seem to be successful at it until an older Black co-worker, Langston, recommends him to use his white voice. Cassius follows the advice and quickly becomes one of the best workers at the company. The "white voice" was perceived as attention-worthy, reassuring, and therefore more likely to lead to sales.

In 2015, Jessica Grose, a *New York Times* journalist and podcast host, confessed that she often received emails complaining about her upspeak that made her sound like a "valley girl".[8] The implication was that she should deepen her voice to please her audience. Five years beforehand, sociologist Ikuko Patricia Yuasa studied a similar phenomenon she called the "creaky voice", now commonly known as the "vocal fry" among young women.[9] You can go on YouTube and type "1 Minute of Kim Kardashian Vocal Fry" in case you don't know what that is. The vocal fry was interpreted as a voice quality of masculinity and authority. Researchers hypothesised that women started using it to deepen their voices and sound more serious or commanding. The vocal fry is one of many strategies used by women to gain legitimacy, a natural response to a perceived lack of assertiveness in the way they present themselves. However, more recent studies have encouraged women to stop using their creaky voice as it makes them sound less competent, trustworthy, educated, attractive, or hireable.[10] So, the use of the vocal fry by women is simultaneously a response to the symbolic violence they face when they accept their status as more fragile individuals, and a new source of mockery.

The second reason why capitalist feminism is not the answer to improve women's conditions in the workplace is that it is rooted in the presumption that a woman's success in life is reduced to her success at work. As Dawn Foster pointed out in *Lean Out*, her response to Sandberg's *Lean In*, capitalist feminists tend to minimise a woman's life to work and having babies. On social media and in the press, women who go back to work just a few days after giving birth are systematically glorified. French right-wing politician Rachida Dati became the centre of attention when she came back to work as Justice Minister only five days after giving birth. Brynn Putnam, the founder of the tech-based fitness company MIRROR, was invited on CNBC to share her journey securing $3 million in funding from her hospital bed, the day her son was born.[11] Foster regretted that Sandberg didn't consider the possibility of an emotional, political, socially engaged life outside work and childbearing. There are, in fact, many forms of work outside the capitalist market: education, volunteering, taking care of one's environment are all valid forms of work. They are just as (if not more) beneficial to society than partaking in what anthropologist David Graeber called "bullshit jobs". Of course, the structure of our economy and the need for financial security makes it hard to step out of a capitalist approach of work. However, we can collectively change that system so that doing so is no longer a privilege but a right.

The third reason why capitalist feminism is not the answer is that having more women leading capitalist companies is not something to celebrate. Liberals often defend the idea that in order to achieve progress and equality, we have to change the system from within. While Sandberg probably wouldn't use those words, she more or less implies the same thing. But can we really break the system from within, one promotion at a time? Asking for a pay rise or promotion requires negotiations which means you must show why *you* deserve it. What extra value did *you* bring to the company? I post videos on a platform that takes 45% of the ad revenue I generate. I think it's unfair, but if I was to go and negotiate with YouTube to get a better percentage, they would probably ask me why they should increase *my* rate in particular. What have I done that would make *me* deserve it? Answering that it simply isn't fair wouldn't work because everybody else is getting the same 55% share of the revenue and isn't complaining. If I said that I bring people to their platform with my videos and other YouTube content I recommend, they would probably answer that other creators do a better job at it than I do. I can't win this battle by myself and, honestly, even if I did, how would I feel knowing that other creators are still not paid fairly? What one can achieve as an individual is very limited compared to what one could achieve as part of a larger structure defending similar interests. That's why unions exist and are so important.

Girlboss Union: An Alternative?

In her book *Make Bosses Pay: Why We Need Unions*, Eve Livingston challenged the idea that unions are for middle-aged white men and invited younger and diverse demographics to join union boards or create one if there aren't any at their workplace. She passionately explained that "a union […] is solidarity, representation, protection, advocacy […] it is hope and optimism, fury, and justice".[12] Eve makes it very clear: it is better to ensure that *one hundred* women employees earn a decent wage rather than getting *one* woman promoted to CEO.

Unions are our best chance at being better compensated for the value we create, at fighting against discrimination, and ensuring job security and fair pay, not just for the few who can ask for it, but for all workers. Unions are also cool now. Some argue they have replaced the girlboss. On January 5, 2022, @pegasiforpoliceabolition tweeted: "Girlboss is over. 2022 is the year of the girlunion". Eve Livingston herself wrote an article aimed at abolishing the girlboss and replacing it with "girlworkers of the girlworld".[13] In it, she argued that women — especially Gen Z and millennial women — are dissatisfied at work and are done with "girlbossing" as the answer to all their problems. Her article follows the 2021 "I don't dream of labor" internet movement which gathered many testimonies of young female workers who didn't want to do the typical 9-5 jobs. The trend did receive its fair share of criticism as, once again, the answer to the problem was often to become a freelancer, to be your own boss, but a good/ethical one! Girlunion therefore seeks to offer an alternative solution. It hopes to channel the feeling of dissatisfaction and desire for change into workers' advocacy. Based on a reappropriation of the term "girlboss", "girlunion" hopes to speak to women working in all sectors of the economy, of all classes and backgrounds. Just like the girlboss, it wants to empower female workers, but unlike the girlboss, it refuses the trickle-down approach of capitalist feminists. In fact, Dawn Foster described Sandberg's *Lean In* as the manifesto of the few. She concluded that "leaning out" of the corporate model is a more effective way of securing change than "leaning in".[14] She wanted to see feminism depart from its liberal, pastel progressive,[15] trickle-down agenda, to go back to the essentials — the recognition and correction of women's material and political disadvantages.[16]

With that goal in mind, girlunion tends to appear as a contradiction. It seeks to make working-class feminism cool by reappropriating what made the girlboss cool. The strategy of using identity (in this case womanhood) as a unioniser has historically been efficient in expanding social movements and making advances. However, identity-based movements often get absorbed by the structures they seek to challenge.

Hashtags like #blacklivesmatter, #bodypositivity and #girlpower found on activists' pages quickly made their way into corporations' advertisement campaigns. Red-washing, as it is now called, uses the language and aesthetics of social movements to attach the appearance of progressivism to a brand. In doing so, corporations turn activism — being a feminist, acting against climate change — into something fun, something one can buy. Maybe you remember the Pepsi campaign where model Kendall Jenner stepped out of a protest to offer a Pepsi can to a police officer, therefore turning Pepsi into a peacemaker. Gillette also encouraged men to turn their back on toxic masculinity as part of their #MeToo inspired campaign. This form of capitalism-friendly progressivism de-radicalises social justice and brings sparkles to activism. The issue isn't so much that it doesn't go far enough — nobody expects a corporation to be radical — but rather that it prevents us from going any further. What I mean by that is that it perpetuates the idea that we can solve everything with ethical capitalism. That ethical capitalism is *the* realistic progressive option.

When I think about girlunion, I think about girlpower meets Rosie the Riveter, a combination that is built to be absorbed by capitalism. *Girl*union kept the infantilising, girly aspect of girlboss, which is something many disliked because of how depoliticising and heteronormative it sounded. Eve Livingston's article on girlunion made it to fashion and culture magazine *i-D*'s Instagram page. What's amusing though is that it follows a post showing the cover of a surprise issue of *i-D* starring the ultimate girlboss, Kim Kardashian, who controversially stated that women don't want to work these days...

While it is a step in the right direction, the girlunion trend might not be relatable to the "99%" of women.[17] That's why Dawn Foster chose to use the phrase "working-class feminism" instead, but again, can a large number of people identify with it? What do we mean by "working-class"? A caregiver living in Liverpool's suburbs will certainly be perceived and surely identify as working class. But what about, let's say, a college-educated librarian living in Dublin? In a passage of *Beautiful World, Where Are You?* Sally Rooney explored what it means to be working-class in the twenty-first century. In it, her character Eileen, a college-educated librarian living in Dublin, assumes that she is working class, to which another character, Gary, bitterly responds that working class is not a fashion but an identity. Eileen then asks him how putting half her income into rent, not owning any property and being exploited by a boss does not make her part of the working class.

If working-class feminism is to grow within the feminist movement and become its main source of inspiration, then it is necessary to expand the definition of what working class is so that more people can identify with it. In France, for instance, our class repartition system incentivises us to identify as middle class. The category of the lower middle-class forces low-income households and some educated workers (like Eileen) to remain in the middle-class bubble. On the other hand, employees whose incomes are high are reluctant to think of themselves as upper class. They prefer the "upper-*middle-*class" label instead. The belief in the existence of an almost all-encompassing middle class, a symbol of social mobility, prevents people who work for a living and see most of their income disappear in the fulfilment of their basic needs from developing a working-class consciousness.

Working-class feminism must also face the reluctance of working-class women to identify as feminists. Such a reluctance is rooted in the fact that the feminist movement has historically been led by bourgeois white women and that is not something working-class women — many being of colour — identify with. The recognition of those intersectional identities within feminism helps break the verticality of the movement and instead promote a collective of differences. In other words, feminism cannot be ambitious if it is not willing to dismantle its own power imbalances.

Unsurprisingly, the corporate world has integrated the concept of intersectionality by providing workshops raising awareness among employees and managers. It conveniently reduces intersectionality to the understanding that people have multi-dimensional identities and that everyone can experience different levels of discrimination based on those identities. But a capitalist-friendly version of intersectionality only helps a selected few join the 1%. That is exactly what happened with girlboss feminism, a movement that encouraged (primarily) white women to join men's circles and become high-earning bosses or managers. It is true that the founder of the concept of intersectionality, Black scholar Kimberlé Crenshaw (abolitionist Sojourner Truth paved the way for the materialisation of the concept when she asked "Ain't I a Woman?" at the Woman's Rights Convention in 1851, therefore highlighting her specific identity as a Black woman[18]), did not really include capitalism and class in her first analysis. However, the feminist thinkers that came before and after her did. The point of intersectionality, they argued, is to help us specify the different forms of oppression individuals face with the goal of dismantling all of them. In other words, true liberation cannot be achieved if only class disparities are eliminated, or if only racial inequalities are cancelled, or if only gender discrimination becomes obsolete. For instance, philosopher Chiara Bottici reminds intersectionality advocates of the long feminist tradition that has consistently advocated for the dismantlement of all forms of domination, what she calls "anarchafeminism".[19]

Socialist feminism, anarchafeminism. These are big scary words that imply it is fruitless to believe we can fix capitalism. But unless we are willing to take those options more seriously, true liberation for all will not happen and all forms of radicality will be progressively absorbed by capitalism.

Pastel Progressivism

In the video in which Kim Kardashian provocatively stated that women in business don't want to put in the work, she and her family members also looked back at what they accomplished with their TV reality show. Kris Jenner stressed that they have been able to shed light on issues like the homeless situation in Los Angeles and prison reform — things that they "actually care about".[20] I'm not here to judge the Kardashians' intentions, but similarly, I'm not here to explain in four paragraphs why all of it sounds quite comical. Political consciousness is now used to divert criticism. It gives the appearance of progressivism. However, it's not because the girlboss is politically conscious that she's not a greedy capitalist anymore.

In December 2021, Molly-Mae Hague, the newly appointed creative director of the fast fashion company PrettyLittleThing, declared on Steven Bartlett's *The Diary of a CEO* podcast that "if you want something enough you can achieve it" as a reply to the criticism she got for saying "we all have the same twenty-four hours in a day". The fact that she was a young woman coming from a TV reality show made the backlash unfairly larger and nastier than what we usually see, but deep down, the criticism was fair. Another young female guest of the podcast was Grace Beverley, who, as the title of the episode indicates, has built "a multi-million-pound empire at age 24". An Oxford graduate and fitgirl (meaning someone for whom fitness and weightlifting are a big part of their lives) turned CEO, she made sure from the beginning that she was going to do things right. As an example, her activewear brand Tala is sustainable and ethically made. On the podcast, Steve Bartlett asked her a bunch of questions that could have turned into a Molly-Mae type of situation: "What are your secrets for success?" "How hard do you work?", etc. Every time, Beverley dodged the easy answer and reminded Bartlett that on top of her hard work, she held a certain amount of privilege and got lucky. Grace Beverley, like many Gen Z and millennial entrepreneurs, are masters of the language of pastel progressivism. They seek to become the most ethical they can be while remaining on *Forbes'* 30 under 30 list.

Pastel progressivism — which can take the form of pink-washing, green-washing, woke-washing, etc. — does not solely manifest itself in the relationship between a company and its customers. It is also reflected in the attitude between employers and employees through red-washing. A common example of such a practice is Canadian corporations' sponsorships of indigenous education, art, or culture to conceal harmful behaviours and their history of colonialism.[21] Today, the definition of red-washing has expanded to refer to the promotion of left-wing values to garner consumers and workers' interest. Indeed, we have reached a point in the history of capitalism where Silicon Valley CEOs talk about how Marxism influences their leadership ethic. Li Jin, a venture capitalist and crypto enthusiast who has built her business around the creator economy, is among those people. In an interview she gave to the *New York Times*, Jin is described as "aggressively pro-worker". She believes that "creators should get the same rights as other workers" and sees the development of cryptocurrencies as a mean to achieve that.[22]

First, if Karl Marx was still alive, I don't think he would be a fan of cryptocurrencies. Second, Li Jin is doing the thing, she is red-washing. If we compare what Li Jin says to what she does, we end up facing many contradictions. During a talk she gave to an audience of start-uppers, investors and creator economy enthusiasts, she stressed how crucial it is to invest in creators and young entrepreneurs.[23] But when we look at the start-ups her venture firm invests in, we realise that most of them are intermediaries —platforms that take a share of creators' revenue, like YouTube, TikTok, Instagram, OnlyFans, etc. So no, she doesn't really care about content creators like me, she wants to pump more money out of us. No power back to the creator, but a successful red-washing attempt.

The crypto community — which Li Jin belongs to and profits from — loves to portray itself as progressive on every level. The most popular cryptocurrency, Bitcoin, was created as a response to the 2008 subprime mortgage crisis. It is a decentralised medium of exchange that seeks to challenge traditional currencies (like USD, GBP, EUR, etc.) regulated by central authorities. Enthusiastic about the crypto utopia, celebrities quickly jumped on the bandwagon and started promoting it. One of the funniest moments of the celebrity crypto craze was Matt Damon's ad for the exchange platform Crypto titled, like the Latin proverb, "Fortune favours the brave", in which the actor compared crypto to space discoveries and what not. Female celebrities also got interested. Reese Witherspoon, Paris Hilton, Gwyneth Paltrow, Katy Perry, Mila Kunis and others pushed women to join the crypto world and invest in NFTs. A NFT (non-fungible token) is a digital asset that can, for example, take the form of a piece of art that one can own, buy and sell like a physical piece of art. In 2021 and 2022, NFTs became a sensation. Every celebrity and their mother had to have one. In interviews and on TV shows, celebrities would show off their NFT apes as if they were the coolest, most avant-gardist people on Earth. For instance, Paltrow and Kunis participated in Zoom meetings in which they offered NFT besties bracelets to participants. Katy Perry also posted on Instagram her time at an FTX event (FTX being one of the leading crypto exchange platforms that filed for bankruptcy in late 2022) shaking hands with Bill Clinton and Tony Blair. She captioned her post as follows:

📢 LISTEN UP LADIES 📢 Did you know that women only make up 7% of the crypto world!? WHY ARE WE SETTLING FOR CRYPTO CRUMBS ⬤ LETS GET THAT BAG OK ▰▰▰#educatebabes #financialliteracy #cryptobahamas[24]

Washington Post journalist Nitasha Tiku called these celebrities "crypto girlbosses".[25] In fact, it appears that most of them were financially compensated for promoting cryptocurrencies and NFTs and/or benefitted from the fact that more people invested in crypto, helping increase its value. Women are not the only group crypto targeted. People of colour, LGBTQ+ people and young working-class people were also encouraged to join and "get that bag". However, the promise of crypto to revolutionise the financial world and give power back to people was only a selling argument. Crypto is deeply unequal because one's power is proportionate to the amount of cryptocurrencies one owns, and guess who have the most? People who had already built their wealth outside of the crypto world — a lot of them coming from Big Tech. So, to sum it up in just a few words: crypto is a libertarian utopia for the already wealthy.[26] The crypto girlbosses, just like other girlbosses, used political consciousness to earn their right to grift. In fact, when NFTs took a hit in 2022 and the crypto market lost momentum, celebrities stopped promoting them altogether. Reese Witherspoon, who had chosen a World of Women NFT as her profile picture on Twitter, switched back to a normal picture of herself and doesn't talk about NFTs on her feed anymore. Kim Kardashian had to pay more than $1 million for failing to disclose a payment she received for touting a crypto asset on Instagram.[27] Finally, FTX was revealed to be a scam. Suddenly, no one wanted to be part of it anymore, but those at the bottom who were told to believe in it heavily paid the price.

To conclude, the *Lean In* girlboss, the politically conscious girlboss, the crypto girlboss, or any [insert adjective] girlboss has been considered the ideal woman since the rise of neoliberalism and will continue to be to some extent. The fact that she is both a productive worker and, at some point in her life, a mother means that she fulfils all the roles that capitalist society expects of her. Millennial and Gen X internet users are the target audience of girlboss content. If you type "millennial aesthetic" on Google, you end up with something that very much resembles the "girlboss aesthetic".

The latter is recognisable by its use of pastel colours, marble and motivational quotes on the planner, the computer home screen, the fridge magnets, the bathroom wallpaper — everywhere. If you still struggle to picture what it looks like, you can have a look at Gwyneth Paltrow's 2022 *Architectural Digest* video on YouTube and your curiosity will be more than satisfied. On the other hand, Gen Z users don't relate as much to the girlboss lifestyle and aesthetic. They were made aware of the toxicity of hustle culture — namely the tendency to glorify productivity and financial success to the point of neglecting one's mental health. But the girlboss cannot disappear, she adapts. Taking into consideration criticism coming from Gen Z users, the new version of the girlboss became more self-care focused. However, the project remains the same: one must become the best version of themselves for personal and career growth.

That Girl and Alternative Self-Help

classical music on

I live in the American Gardens Building on W. 81st Street on the 11th floor. My name is Patrick Bateman. I'm 27 years old. I believe in taking care of myself, and a balanced diet, and a rigorous exercise routine. In the morning, if my face is a little puffy, I put on an icepack while doing my stomach crunches. I can do a thousand now. After I remove the ice pack, I use a deep pore cleanser lotion. In the shower, I use a water-activated gel cleanser. Then, a honey almond body scrub, and on the face, an exfoliating gel scrub. Then I apply an herb-mint facial mask which I leave on for ten minutes while I prepare the rest of my routine. I always use an after-shave lotion with little or no alcohol, because alcohol dries your face out, and makes you look older. Then moisturizer, then an anti-aging eye balm followed by a final moisturizing protective lotion.

Bret Easton Ellis, *American Psycho*

lo-fi music on

Hi guys! My name's Amanda, I'm twenty-four, I live in a studio in New York, in the West Village to be more specific, and today I want to show you my morning routine. I really believe in taking care of myself, being healthy, and working out every day. I always put my workout clothes next to my bed so that I'm reminded in the morning that I need to exercise. I quickly put them on, head to the kitchen to fill up my water bottle and add a little bit of lemon to boost my metabolism. Then, it's time to work out. I do a series of core exercises, glutes exercises, a little bit of cardio, and always finish with fifteen minutes of meditation. After I roll up my yoga mat, I go take a shower, exfoliate my skin, and move on to skincare. I started using anti-aging serums last year, so I apply some on my face, as well as a light moisturiser with SPF50, and then do a light makeup. You guys say I don't need it, but I never know who I might meet today! Once that is done, I head back to the kitchen to prepare breakfast. I like to make porridge with plant milk, add berries, and a spoon of peanut butter on top. I sometimes treat myself with an extra fruit as a reward for not using my phone yet! Finally, before work starts, I sit down with my breakfast and a journal in front of the window, and write down my intentions for the day, as well as what I'm grateful for.

Lifestyle content is one of the most popular genres on social media. Judging from the content of the comment sections, it appears that women are more likely to watch it and have their tastes and beliefs influenced by it. I'm one of these women. I grew up watching a *lot* of lifestyle content, including *that girl* influencers. Just like Patrick Bateman in *American Psycho*, *that girl* is the personification of self-discipline and success. She prioritises taking great care of herself to maintain an image of perfection. Waking up early, working out, reading, eating healthy, consuming responsibly, journaling, developing artistic hobbies, being productive, being financially literate, having a large social circle as well as dedicated "me-time" — these are all elements that define *that girl*'s daily life. Online tutorials on how to become *that girl* gather millions of views, meaning it is more than just a trend. A significant amount of Gen Z and millennial women recognise or want to recognise themselves in her.

At first glance, the trend appears rather inoffensive. *That girl* is about building better habits, taking care of oneself, and feeling more confident in one's body. Nevertheless, it happens to simultaneously be one of the most popular and most criticised internet aesthetics of our generation. It is said that she sets unachievable standards for women, that the degree of productivity and self-control she showcases cannot be sustained long-term. For some, *that girl* is the female version of the *hustle bro*, a phrase which defines men who centre their identity on their capacity to work hard and be self-disciplined in the pursuit of financial freedom. For others she is the twenty-first-century version of the Stepford wife. Indeed, *that girl*'s focus on self-mastery makes her part of the self-help genre that is based on a combination of psychological and philosophical precepts applicable to the goal of personal growth. However, *that girl* is different from the typical *hustle bro* because each of them take part in the world of self-help according to their gender and the norms associated with it. Self-care doesn't have the same meaning for someone socialised as a man as it does for a woman. Self-care gives respectability to a man, but ultimately achievements and material possessions are what make him "high value". For women, self-care and looks are what primarily gives her value. A woman who doesn't take care of herself is not girlfriend- or wife-material because she doesn't make herself desirable for men.

Another difference between *that girl* and *the hustle bro* is that the first one is more likely to envision well-being as an end in itself, whereas the second one is ultimately seeking financial success. *That girl* rarely discusses finances, and when she does, the backlash can get intense. For a little while, female lifestyle influencers living in big cities took part in the "what I spend in a week as a twenty-something year old in [insert trendy city]" challenge. In it, they vlogged their week and recorded all their expenses to finally add them up and feel bad for not saving more money. Many viewers saw it as a display of a privileged lifestyle and did not like it. Several thrifty finance bros also capitalised on the challenge by monetising reaction videos mocking the women's supposed lack of responsibility. It was interesting to see that most of these women's expenses were, as it happens, related to their jobs as *that girl* influencers — sustaining a healthy diet, a gym membership, buying expensive clothing and make-up, going out for video content, or simply paying rent in a trendy city. It was also comical to see finance bros mansplain to these women that they needed to buy less matcha lattes, while they spend a disproportionate amount of money on expensive cars and watches.

That girl is a soft girlboss who doesn't buy the stereotypically masculine hustle mentality but prioritises healthy productivity. Being *that girl* is a way to remain competitive in the market of individuals while preventing it from harming one's mental health. That is why she is part of a genre I call "alternative self-help" — a form of self-help that is critical of the damaging effects of hustle culture but doesn't fully give up on it. Alternative self-help appears as the "feminine" version of the toxic world of hustle culture, as self-care, a supposedly feminine quality, is central to it. While the typical girlboss directs her energy outwards for competition and growth, *that girl* feels the need to reconnect with her feminine self. Her withdrawal into the self entails a disconnection from the world, community and politics. In that sense, she remains a product of neoliberalism — the embodiment of the apolitical or blissful individualist.[28]

Now, I want to look more closely at the notion of self-care. Self-care has always been an essential component of self-help. Samuel Smiles' book *Self-Help* is arguably the ancestor of the genre. Published in 1859, it aligned with mid-Victorian ideals of self-reliance and respectability as moral virtues. The book was acclaimed by wealthy entrepreneurs,[29] and trashed by leftists[30] — nothing has changed, really. In it, the author wrote about money, energy and courage, men of business, and the notion of *character*. It is through this very notion of character that self-care is mobilised. Early on, self-help gurus established character as a pillar of success. Liberalism was the promise of class mobility for all, and one's appearance in public had to reflect one's desire to climb the social ladder.

In 1901, Booker T. Washington published his autobiography *Up from Slavery*, tracing his journey from being an enslaved child to the creation of the Tuskegee Institute educating Black youth and helping them rise in society. Like Samuel Smiles, Washington promoted respectability as a tool for social mobility. Contrary to Smiles' book, however, *Up from Slavery* was not a manual for personal success, it was a manifesto for the emancipation of the African American community. Black leaders including W.E.B Du Bois and Marcus Garvey also encouraged Black folks to develop *character* by taking care of their bodies with daily practices.[31] Washington promoted "The Gospel of the Toothbrush",[32] while Du Bois focused on that of "soap and water".[33] A lack of hygiene was notable in the early nineteenth century, it was not a Black people's problem only. For African Americans, taking care of oneself, both physically and mentally, was about forging strong emancipated bodies that commanded white people's respect and could help forge a Black nation.

These ideas were inspired by Ancient Greek philosophers, especially Socrates and Plato, who wrote and talked about the philosophy of self-knowledge. Like Du Bois, Socrates regularly stopped young people to tell them to take care of themselves. He blamed them for "devoting all [their] care to increasing [their] wealth, reputation and honors while not caring for even considering [their] reason, truth and the constant improvement of [their] soul".[34] In *The Hermeneutics of the Subject*, philosopher Michel Foucault revisited Socrates and Plato to better understand what they meant by the well-known precept "know yourself" — which self-help gurus live by. He realised that the expression was related to a different concept also found in ancient texts: *epimeleia heautou*, "care of oneself". According to Foucault, *epimeleia heautou* is an attitude towards the self, others and the world. This notion was used by Socrates, who advised young ambitious men to work on themselves before they took on political roles and became accountable to the people.[35] It could be argued that African American leaders like Du Bois mobilised this philosophy when they promoted the care of one's body and mind to uplift their race. Sure, the onus is first put on the individual, but it extends far beyond it.

It is tempting to compare the goal of *epimeleia heautou* to the goal of alternative self-help. However, it is crucial not to confuse the care of oneself with the postmodern individualist's obsession with self-actualisation.[36] In other words, contemporary self-help utilises ancient philosophy of self-knowledge for self-actualisation. But by doing so, it completely misses the point. It subverted its initial goal, which was to help people become well-rounded, self-aware individuals ready to become citizens and therefore political actors. Today, taking care of oneself only serves to improve one's brand in the market of individuals. The built-in outwardness of ancient self-care practices has been entirely redirected onto the self.

Going back to the introductory passages comparing Patrick Bateman and a fictional *that girl*, we see that taking care of oneself is translated into a set of practices applied to the body and mind. The self by the self, Foucault argues, are the "actions by which one takes responsibility for oneself, and by which changes, purifies, transforms, and transfigures oneself".[37] He defined those practices as "techniques of the self". Among them are meditation, memorisation of the past, and examination of conscientiousness, what we would now probably refer to as mindfulness. (Ancient self-help guru) Plutarch went as far as recommending you try the following exercise:

You start the morning with a series of lengthy, difficult, and tiring physical exercises, which give you an appetite. Having done this, you have sumptuous tables served with extraordinarily rich dishes filled with the most attractive food. You place yourself before them, gaze on them, and meditate. Then you call the slaves. You give this food to the slaves and content yourself with their extremely frugal food.[38]

Such extravagances, that only constitute one part of the project that is *epimeleia heautou*, became the norm in the realm of online self-help. Nowadays, self-help gurus, including *that girl*, recommend you take cold showers right after you wake up (at 5am preferably), fast till 12pm, do 10k steps every day, stop using social media for a month, check stocks performances while you go to the loo and whatnot. One challenge that I kept hearing about was to go to a coffee shop and ask for a discount on your coffee. How brave!

Making fun of self-help is very easy and strangely very enjoyable, especially as someone who has followed some of these extravagant practices. Consistently maintaining such levels of self-discipline creates a sense of moral superiority. However, that is precisely what led Socrates to recommend young and proud Alcibiades to "know himself". By that he meant that one's relationship to oneself is reflected in one's relationship to others. Knowing oneself meant understanding one's inferiority, one's skills, one's prejudices and working on them to become a better person — for others. Again, those principles have been incorporated into capitalist culture through the figure of the alternative self-help guru who talks openly about failure, rejection and doubt in order to appear more authentic to their audience. Once the guru has gathered enough people around his personality to build a profitable fanbase, they can perpetuate the values or system they incarnate.

That girl is at the intersection of two systems: neoliberalism (alternative self-help) and patriarchy (patriarchal femininity). Both systems are internalised from a very young age so that what *that girl* stands for sounds like what we should all naturally stand for. As Foucault demonstrated, we are conditioned to be self-disciplined by the structures that surround us and learn how to value them throughout our lives.[39] In secondary school, I had to stand up when the teacher came in and wait for them to ask us to sit down; a huge timetable was pinned on the wall to structure our day; the bell would ring every hour. This description may sound unsurprisingly familiar to you, and that is precisely what Foucault meant when he said that liberal societies heavily rely on people's internalised discipline to function. Conforming to those rules comes with a reward: good grades, diplomas, a promising career, a nice suburban house, a nuclear family... or a lot of views on your latest morning routine video.

People online are obsessed with routines. Add the word "productive" in the title and you get even more views. The execution of routines is, as we have just described, part of the self-care project. However, it also serves another function, that of increasing one's moral capital. As an example, Jordan B. Peterson has popularised the imperative "clean your room" as a rule for life to which he assigned a moral value. The idea is that if someone cannot even clean their room, they cannot be of any value to society — micro actions have macro impacts. As a matter of fact, every *that girl* morning routine starts with the influencer opening their curtains and making their bed. Those activities performed one after the other, in the same order (as it was rendered in the introductory passage) are easily identifiable by the viewer and signal the accumulation of small productive tasks. Every one of those activities has a moral value attached to it. What is productive, challenging, out of one's comfort zone is good, the rest is bad. Taking a cold shower after waking up at 5am is good. It becomes a symbol of moral virtue, of character and respectability. *That girl* perpetuates this mode of thinking and turns it into a philosophy of life: self-reliance. She finds meaning in short-term and long-term achievements, in the belief that being productive is morally right.

Self-discipline brings success, and success brings happiness. That is the path that was established for us, and we are guilty of reasserting it by systematically validating those who follow it with likes, views, comments, reviews, etc. *We* created *that girl.* We created her according to the structures we have internalised and have learned to value. Across all social media platforms, *that girl* influencers are scrutinised. They are forced to share every single aspect of their daily lives, their morning and night-time routines, including what they eat in a day and what their workouts consist of. *That girl* influencers find themselves in a situation where they must constantly maintain those routines to be able to produce content according to the external gaze's demands. Performing perfection is part of their brand and is necessary for them to survive on the online scene. We are, without always realising it, the pressuring external gaze.

At the end of the eighteenth century, the philosopher and social theorist Jeremy Bentham made a series of social and legal proposals to the British aristocracy, including the introduction of a revolutionary, cost-effective prison project: the panopticon. What makes the panopticon a revolutionary penitentiary is its structure. Built in a circular form, the panopticon contains one single security tower, placed in the middle, and surrounded at a distance by inmates' cells. The central position of the tower meant that a single guard could see all the cells from one standpoint. On the other hand, inmates couldn't tell if the guard, the external gaze, was looking at them or not — they were in a constant state of surveillance. Foucault saw in Bentham's panopticon a metaphor of the rise of the modern disciplinary society.[40]

He argued that institutions like schools, prisons, hospitals, etc., participated in internalising discipline in order to create "docile bodies" through permanent surveillance.

There was of course no way of knowing whether you were being watched at any given moment ... you had to live ... in the assumption that every sound you made was overheard, and, except in darkness, every movement scrutinised.

George Orwell, *1984*

Discussions around the existence of a surveillance state are not taken very seriously in the West because a liberal surveillance society sounds like an oxymoron. However, the concept of the panopticon is very much applicable to our neoliberal societies. Mark Zuckerberg, a twenty-first-century Jeremy Bentham, has created a panopticon out of Facebook and Instagram. These social media platforms were based on the ideal of connecting people all over the world, but their goal now is rather to stimulate and scrutinise users' engagement to please advertisers. According to philosopher Byung-Chul Han, we now live in a digital panopticon where participants "actively communicate with each other and willingly expose themselves".[41] Han's "digital Big Brother" outsources operations (likes, comments, shares) to users in the form of unbounded freedom and communication. As a result, our subjectivity is forged and checked by others — the external gaze.

The online world magnifies phenomena that already exist outside of it. Sociologist David Riesman noticed the appearance of a new "cultural type" in the 1950s that he called "other-directedness". In his book *The Lonely Crowd*, Riesman distinguished three different cultural types: tradition-directedness, inner-directedness and other-directedness. Tradition-directedness refers to individuals who place family, religion and local traditions at the core of their identity. Inner-directedness refers to people who are quite confident, self-reliant, and are able to detach themselves from other people's opinions. Finally, other-directed individuals are usually socially and geographically mobile and define themselves through the way others live. The malleability of this cultural type echoes a desire to gain approval from others. The other-directed individual constantly needs reassurance that others can relate to them. Unsurprisingly, Riesman argued that this last cultural type has become dominant in our culture.

It is necessary to emphasise that other-directedness is not a personality trait, it's a *cultural* type. It's not something that goes from the inside-out, but rather from the outside-in. One's social environment plays a significant role in defining one's cultural type and the homogenization of cultures into the Western so-called "melting pot" naturally fosters a convergence towards one specific type. In fact, Riesman placed the rise of other-directed individuals in the larger context of post-war consumer society. Newly born suburbs were a fertile ground for its development. What people consumed or talked about on TV forged the white middle class's identity, tastes and norms. The structure of suburbs encouraged neighbours to regularly check on each other, correct, conform themselves — their beliefs, their gender expression, their consumption habits, the greenness and height of their lawn — and reinforce their group identity in the process. Those same processes accelerate online because of the constant surveillance of the digital panopticon. Regarding gender expression, both femininity and masculinity are constrained to a given set of characteristics regulated by the external gaze. In the second part of this book, we will delve into masculinity, but for now, let's stick with femininity.

The way gender expression is regulated online is vicious. On the one hand, it allows for a degree of variability, but on the other hand, it systematically excludes from the realm of womanhood those who do not conform to patriarchal femininity. In other words, what it means to be a woman is so constrained that any minor stylistic or behavioural divergence triggers suspicion and can force you out of the box. On the internet, there are many Reddit posts or Quora pages titled "is [insert celebrity name] non-binary/gay?" based on the way certain celebrities present. Interestingly, those posts are often created by queer people seeking to find representation in the media. Because of that, many chose to closely conform, to stay in the box, and avoid speculation. In fact, *that girl* conforms more than she challenges those gender norms. She is the ideal woman according to patriarchal standards. Aesthetically speaking, her make-up and looks are only meant to enhance healthy habits that already show on the outside. The emphasis is put on skincare and a minimal glowy makeup that highlights natural, genetic beauty. Obviously, not everyone can be *that* (clean) *girl* — acne-prone skin get you erased from the list, unattractive facial features, too. A clean girl is more likely to be a young, thin, white woman than a woman of colour. The trend intersects in many ways with the "French girl aesthetic", built on the stereotype of the effortlessly pretty, casually elegant French woman.

Despite appearances, *that girl* is still expected to dedicate a lot of time to maintenance. Beauty writer Arabelle Sicardi wrote that, "men want beauty but they don't want to see the work; they don't want to see the space beauty takes".[42] Achieving and maintaining natural beauty is an investment that women have been conditioned to do for centuries. Clothes, shoes, lingerie, skincare, nails, make-up, hair, but also contraceptive pills, hair removal products, tampons or period pads, etc. Money aside, it is a huge time investment as well. For example, if I continue to wax my legs for the next forty years of my life, I will spend a total of 1000 hours doing that very task (you are right, no girlboss should tolerate such a waste of time). And still, I'm lucky to conform to white beauty standards, meaning that the time and money I spend in maintenance is less important than other women who do not conform to them.

To conclude, *that girl* materialises a white, bourgeois and heteronormative type of femininity. The internalisation of gender norms is reflected in the way the external gaze (viewers, followers, strangers) validates *her* more than any other types of femininity. *That girl* is heralded as the ideal woman, and *that girl* influencers as lifestyle gurus. She uses self-care for self-reliance and to enhance desirability. We, the external gaze, created *that girl* in a way that ensures a long life for both patriarchy and capitalism.

Throughout this chapter, we have shown how the girlboss adapts to criticism from the left by appearing more politically conscious; and from the right by complying with social norms regarding marriage, motherhood, femininity, etc. Ultimately, unless we dismantle the systems that created her, the "basic human needs to get out of the house, be part of the world, speak up and have people listen to you, and recognise you, and appreciate you"[43] will only make her stronger, since the workplace — the preferred avenue to exert that human need — abides by a culture of domination. There now seems to be a consensus around the disliking of the girlboss, even the softer ones like *that girl*. At the moment, the usual line of attack is anti-capitalistic. Criticisms are rooted in growing anti-work sentiments born out of the realisation that capitalist work is not liberating. However, the analysis of *that girl* reminds us that it is not *just* about work and capitalism; it is also about gender and patriarchy. Reducing the issue of the girlboss to capitalism is flawed since it assumes that the culture of domination is a product of capitalism, which is only partly true. Unequal power dynamics between people of various genders or ethnicities can exist outside of capitalism. And refusing to consider this reality can become detrimental, as we will see in the next chapter.

Chapter 2
Traditional Femininity Is
Making a Comeback

#TraditionalLiving as Counterculture

Ideal womanhood is built on difference, what a woman *is not*. In *The Second Sex*, Simone de Beauvoir argued that men are considered as the default gender and that women have sexually connoted gender signifiers. Lipstick, makeup and tight clothes are understood as signs that a woman is sexually aroused. Some men even translate these signs into an invitation to engage in sexual activity with them.[1] Asserting that only women display sexually connoted gender signifiers infers that women are responsible for the sexual arousal of men. In France, in 2020, then Minister of National Education, Jean-Michel Blanquer, demanded that students wear a "republican"[2] outfit after controversies around teenage girls wearing crop tops at school.[3] The message is clear: the ideal (republican) woman must be as modest as possible. What she can be is rather defined by what she cannot be, cannot wear, or cannot show.

The ideal woman, as described by so-called "real" men, is not the same as in that *BuzzFeed* video I watched as a teenager. She is not defined by sexual appeal but rather by the way she should conduct herself. According to them, the ideal woman doesn't have an Instagram account,[4] she ought to be seen but not heard, she's traditionally feminine, she's submissive, she shuts up when asked to. These statements were found in video clips of the self-advertised number one men's podcast in the world, *Fresh and Fit*, which seeks to "provide the TRUTH to Females, Fitness, and Finances". *Fresh and Fit* has more than one million subscribers and more than 300 million views on YouTube. In the *Fresh and Fit* recording studio, you see the two male hosts, Myron Gaines and Fresh Prince CEO, at the forefront, with women closely sitting next to each other around a U-shaped table. The women don't talk much. They are primarily invited on for their sexual appeal in exchange for exposure. Gaines, the most talkative and outrageous of the two hosts, regularly tells these women that they are not marriage material, either because their body count (their number of previous sexual partners) is too high, or because they are seeking too much attention from men. On the contrary, he believes men need to find a girlfriend or wife that will obey them, that won't humiliate them and their legacy. He asserted in one episode that he would be willing to leave the US to find what he wants, implying that Western women are too difficult, too conscious.

In the process of defining ideal femininity to their (primarily heterosexual male) audience, the hosts of *Fresh and Fit* also speak both indirectly and directly to heterosexual women. Indirectly because male viewers come to the podcast to seek *the truth on females* and could then expect their current or future girlfriend to do what the hosts say. And directly because women, to a lesser degree, also watch/listen to *Fresh and Fit*, and could understand what Myron says as what is expected from them. As a matter of fact, a growing community of women has taken on the role of restoring submissive femininity. Among them, #tradwives are teaching women how to become traditional, respectable, and look affluent to attract the right man. Anna Bey, known on YouTube as the person behind *The School of Affluence*, has turned this trend into her brand. Bey went from living the jet-set life, being invited to yacht parties alongside celebrities like Paris Hilton,[5] to launching her first course, "The 7-Step Formula to High Society". In it, she shows women how they can utilise their appearance and attitude to rise in society. T-shirts, cartoon prints, yoga pants and sportswear are a no-no for Anna.

When asked about what made her blow up so quickly, Bey replies that she was the first one to offer this sort of content online. Finishing schools (some call them etiquette schools or charm schools) have existed for centuries, were highly concentrated in the Geneva region in Switzerland, and were attended by members of the aristocracy, the new American elite, models, and actresses. Anna Bey saw an opportunity in democratising finishing schools to aspiring ladies. She opened the doors of those secret elite institutions for women of all backgrounds and ethnicities seeking a traditional lifestyle.

Tradwife content is now very popular on social media, with influencers making tutorials on how to cook and how to dress, sharing their daily lives, taking care of their boyfriends, husbands and children. It remains a niche, but one that attracts a lot of attention. Tradwives have appeared on the TV show *This Morning* and on the BBC in the UK, as well as in articles from various publications including *CNN*, the *Daily Mail* and *Libération* in France. Estée, from the TikTok account @esteecwilliams, is among the tradwives who have made it to the big publications. On her account, Estée provides tutorials, daily routines, and regularly answers viewers' comments. In a TikTok video scoring half a million views and titled "What it means to be a tradwife", Estée explained that this lifestyle is her choice. She's not advocating for women to go back to the kitchen but is only sharing her life. "It's 2022", she says, "women should have the choice to be homemakers or not". Another influential tradwife called Alena Kate Pettit argued on *This Morning* that she is "a feminist because [she] believe[s] feminism to be about choices".[6] The autonomy these women have in choosing to stay at home cannot be taken away from them. As video essayist oliSUNvia showed, saying that these women are brainwashed is both unproductive and alienating.[7] It is interesting, however, to dwell a little on this notion of autonomy, since it is systematically used by tradwives every time they are criticised for being submissive.

Autonomy and choice have been at the core of the women's rights movement, specifically because it served to assert subjectivity. Every time a woman chooses what she wants to do with her life and her body, she reclaims her subjectivity. When a tradwife declares she wants to stay at home, she also reclaims her subjectivity. She benefits from the achievements of the feminist movement and even sets herself up as a product of feminism. "Choice feminism", as it is often called, has become the dominant framework through which people talk about feminism. However, the way it is used by certain groups, including conservative women, as "it's my choice, end of the conversation", often shuts the door for uncomfortable yet necessary conversations. It tends to foster the depoliticization of the personal.[8]

"The personal is political" is a phrase that characterises the US second wave of feminism and is now used by various social movements. It emerged at a time when feminists sought to challenge the nuclear family and the domestic role of women. Essentially, it means that women's issues in the private sphere, like unequal housework or responsibility for childcare, are political issues. More broadly, "the personal is political" helped women understand that the limitations they put on how they want to live their lives, how they want to dress, what sort of job they can do, are all conditioned by the patriarchy. The message sought to be universal, but it wasn't so much in practice. Some women couldn't relate to the white, educated, middle-class feminists who were part of the movement, others didn't have the means to step out of their oppression, and finally, many were satisfied with the way they were. Frustrated by that resistance, some second-wave feminists started investigating the private lives of women, even when they weren't invited to. In *A Decolonial Feminism*, journalist Françoise Vergès coined the phrase "civilisational feminism" to refer to those feminists who sought to impose their vision of feminism onto other groups of women. In particular, she looked at how the MFPF (*Mouvement Français pour le Planning Familial*, the French Movement for Planned Parenthood) spoke to French Muslim women to "call on [their] lucidity" and "courage" and abandon the hijab.[9] Civilisational feminism is no longer tolerated in progressive feminist circles because it doesn't consider the diversity of women. It has been rightly discredited by the works of marginalised feminist scholars including — but not limited to — bell hooks. It is now deemed inappropriate to impose one's experience of feminism onto other women. There is not one feminism but various feminisms, and that is a good thing.

If we go back to the problem described earlier, namely that choice feminism depoliticises the personal, we now understand that the answer to that problem cannot be a return to top-down civilisational feminism. It is essential not to compromise a woman's right to choose, even if it does not align with one's supposedly objective experience of feminism. However, we cannot stop there. For when we look at the way women talk about choice feminism, we understand that "choice", and not the *outcome of that choice*, has become the locus of liberation. It implies that we have entered a post-feminist era where women's liberation is granted by their right to choose for themselves.[10] In that case, choice feminism happens to be just as elitist as civilisational feminism, because it neglects the fact that many women do not have the ability to choose or are constrained by external forces. For that reason, reducing feminism to the ability to choose is dangerously flawed. Choice is a modality through which women can potentially achieve liberation, but it is crucial to state that choice does not necessarily equal liberation. Choice is not an end in itself.

Nonetheless, traditional influencers do describe their choice to stay at home as liberating, a source of happiness. In a TikTok video that went viral, @justpearlythings interviewed a tradwife who asked "When you think about it, you submit to your boss to make you clean stupid shelves at your retail job, right? But wouldn't it be better if you were cleaning your own shit?"[11]

Such an observation had already been shared by Christian writer G.K. Chesterton in 1927, when he said that birth control "is mixed up with a muddled idea that women are free when they serve their employers but slaves when they help their husbands".[12] The argument that going back to traditional living is a form of resistance against the exploitative nature of work under capitalism is now commonly used by online conservatives. For instance, in mid-2022, groups of internet users circulated the idea that women's liberation was a plot meant to tax the other half of the population. It originated from an interview that Alex Jones (the serial conspiracist behind the "free speech" far-right news service *InfoWars*) conducted in 2009 with Aaron Russo, a friend of Nick Rockefeller, a member of the Rockefeller family, one of the richest and most powerful families in the world and the frequent subject of conspiracy theories. Russo recounted a conversation he had with Rockefeller in which he allegedly admitted that his family funded feminist organisations to tax women in the workforce.[13] I remember receiving several comments alluding to this allegation under some of my videos, which made me realise how widespread it was. People said that feminism was the biggest scam in history, that the alliance of feminism and neoliberalism had enslaved humanity. I was sceptical because I knew that Ronald Reagan, a neoliberal advocate himself, was opposed to the idea of encouraging women into the workforce. He even connected rising unemployment figures to women's participation in the workforce when he said, "it is the great increase of the people going into the job market, and — ladies, I'm not picking on anyone but — because of the increase in women who are working today".[14] Nevertheless, what seemed to be a conspiracy theory kept growing. A dramatic TikTok video made by @shannen.micheal (who also shares information on why veganism is a scam, why you should invest in NFTs, and why you should let your genitals absorb the energy of the sun), retold the Russo/Rockefeller story with screenshots of unsourced articles and apocalyptic music in the background. The video was seen more than four million times.

Conspiracy theory aside, it is necessary to highlight that the rejection of the neoliberal "career woman" by tradfluencers is coherent with the rise of anti-work sentiments. In 2021, young (mostly) female workers shared online that they "don't dream of labor" or that they "don't have a dream job". They wished they could reject the typical 9-5 job, invest their time in something meaningful, explore their creativity, and enjoy slow living. Others soon joined the trend by sharing their own experience, turning "I don't dream of labor" into a viral internet movement. Since then, the topic of anti-work has remained popular online and is no longer gatekept by left-wing content creators. Women now widely understand that the workplace isn't exactly where liberation is to be found. Work under capitalism is exploitative. The girlboss is not liberated, she's a slave to the system. For decades, feminists have encouraged women to take back power by adapting to men's environments, by going into debt to pay for an education and working hard to compete in a system rigged against them. We called it liberation. Many women are coming to the realisation that they don't *feel* liberated.

The death of the girlboss leaves a space for someone or something to reclaim what liberation means. Unsurprisingly, traditional living influencers are in the process of doing just that. Many of them have already shared how their former lives as career women did not suit them, they felt it was forced on them and did not align with their true nature. Tradwife Alena Kate Pettitt said to the BBC that being a tradwife felt right to her. She now has the time to cook for herself and her family, to see friends and to have hobbies. She looks very fulfilled, *liberated*, one could say. Under the TikTok videos of tradwives, women comment how they wished they had time to relax, prepare their own meals and be creative. Traditional living content has become a form of escapism for many women who are not fulfilled at work. Progressively, tradfluencers reverse the dichotomy popularised by the feminist movement, namely that "domesticity equals oppression" and "work equals liberation".

As a matter of fact, radical feminists have always condemned the nuclear family as the locus of women's oppression. African American poet and feminist Pat Parker said that "as long as women are bound by the nuclear family structure, we cannot effectively move towards revolution".[15] Under capitalism, liberation from the nuclear family became synonymous with forging financial independence. Feminists encouraged young women to go to college and get a job so that they could more easily step out of oppressive and sometimes violent relationships. Still today, according to the World Health Organization, almost one third of women have been subjected to some form of physical and/or sexual violence by their intimate partner. Pro-work incentives were successful since women now make the majority of bachelor graduates in a wide variety of fields.[16] But with the rise of neoliberalism in the 1980s, reaching financial independence was no longer described as a tool of safety but rather as an assertion of individual power. On the other hand, being a housewife became increasingly uncool. In one of her podcast episodes, Mikhaila Peterson (the daughter of Jordan), who chose to be a stay-at-home wife, complained that she was looked down upon by her neighbours and friends for having a kid so young and choosing a traditional lifestyle. She felt like mothers were not valued as much as they used to be. She nevertheless concluded the episode with optimism: "I feel like things are changing".[17] In fact, she is not completely wrong. Tradfluencers tell us that if being a girlboss is no longer coded as liberation, then liberation ought to be found in traditional living.

It is not usual to hear mainstream feminists bring up the topic of housewives. In one of her podcast episodes, French feminist Louise Aubery, known as MyBetterSelf, regretted that the girlboss had been idolised at the expense of the stay-at-home mother.[18] It is interesting to me to see how Louise was naturally drawn to that comparison, as if these two options represented both ends of the same spectrum — that of a woman's realm of possibility. It is precisely the existence of this rigid binary that allows for the comeback of traditional living. Many women, like Aubery, have internalised that the possibilities they have are limited. That is why we see former career women switch to traditional living as the only alternative they can envision. In the process of glamorising girlbossing as liberation, we have failed to build a popular alternative to this binary. We have systematically reduced a woman's life to work under capitalism and domesticity.

Why is there such a binary? In fact, we could already rejoice at the existence of a binary choice. For a long time, women whose husbands could support them were reduced to the domestic sphere. Domesticity never fully disappeared from women's lives. Working women continue to do most of the housework, and upper-class women only relegate that task to working-class women. The patriarchal capitalist system gives the illusion that women can escape their "natural" domestic role through work when, in fact, they are constantly drawn back to it. That is why socialist and anarchist feminists refuse to see patriarchy as an entity operating outside capitalism, like liberal feminists tend to do. Their alternative to the binary was and is to liberate workers from capitalist modes of production, including the free domestic work that women provide. Because of online tradwives, it is now difficult to frame domesticity as something inherently oppressive because they look so happy and fulfilled. After all, isn't that the goal of feminism? To ensure women live happy and fulfilling lives? Am I imposing what my vision of a liberated feminism is onto them? Well, it is most likely to be the other way around.

The revival of traditional living as a form of counterculture is mediated by a specific type of women, mostly white, middle- to upper-middle class women who have either achieved financial freedom in a former career and can rely on their husband's income to support them, or who have built a business around traditional living, like Anna Bey, Alena Kate Pettitt and many others. This reality is reflected in the aesthetic these women portray. Tradwife content online is an almost perfect reproduction of the 1950s representations of the nuclear families in TV ads and magazines — the "she'll be happier with a hoover" housewife. Tradfluencers have revived a commercial aesthetic that they understood as an accurate depiction of domesticity.

However, it is not because it depicts a privileged lifestyle that the tradwife trend is irrelevant. Traditional living influencers benefit from the fact that online aesthetics are decreasingly gatekept by the group they originate from. By that I mean that an aesthetic like dark academia — which seeks inspiration from Oxbridge and Ivy League universities — can be reclaimed by people who are generally excluded from these wealthy, educated spheres. The aesthetic becomes a cosplay, almost a game. In an article for the *Daily Mail*, several tradwives, including Alena Kate Pettitt, seemed to have fun dressing up as 1950s housewives with old home appliances.[19] TikToker Estée, who we mentioned earlier, chose an aesthetic that merges the 1950s Stepford wife with Marilyn Monroe. In one of her videos, YouTuber Teya, known as StrangeAeons, also explored how cottagecore became synonymous with traditional living using the concept of the content pipeline. Social media pipelines refer to the movement of content consumption based on users' preferences, which can lead to some forms of radicalisation. StrangeAeons looked at a possible social media pipeline: the #cottagecore to #tradwife one. Cottagecore is an aesthetic that emerged in the last decade and centres around farm life, growing your own food, making your own clothes and living in the countryside. She noticed on Tumblr that a number of posts with pictures of women wearing long dresses in nature used a range of hashtags, including #cozyaesthetic, #cottagecore, #cottagelife, #homesteading, #tradwife, #traditionalfeminity and #traditionalgenderroles. She also discovered another post with similar hashtags, similar pictures and an additional text this time, written by a new tradwife who enthusiastically shared her lifestyle. In other words, a Tumblr user searching for posts on #cottagecore can easily end up on a post promoting #traditionalgenderroles.[20] This particular pipeline can be reproduced on image-based social media platforms used by Gen Z and millennial women, including Instagram and TikTok, to the point where cottagecore starts to signal traditional living.

Traditional living advocates restore domesticity as something *all* women can enjoy. They become the spokespersons of a group of women they frame as looked down upon, the stay-at-home girlfriends and wives, and attract media sympathy because of that. The fact that they are members of the middle and upper middle-class allows them to occupy a space online at the expense of other classes of women, specifically working-class women, for whom domesticity is rarely happy and liberating.[21] However, it is precisely its traditional language and aesthetic that continues to keep most female online users away from it. The promotion of strict gender roles is not compatible with liberal audiences.

To attract a broader audience, traditional living had to adopt a different language.

Divine Femininity

Divine femininity relates back to the Egyptian goddess Isis, Greek goddesses Gaïa and Aphrodite, or Hindu goddess Shakti. It has become extremely popular on social media as it is connected to new age spirituality. Perceived as the grouping of incorruptible forces operating above and within human beings, new age spirituality is used by its advocates to make sense of the world and the self. It conveniently turns into something that cannot be political/politicised because it is said to be based on universal natural laws. New age spirituality is therefore applied to various fields like finance, health and relationships with the purpose of camouflaging any possible bias. That is precisely what divine femininity does with gender essentialism.

Divine femininity influencers educate their audience on how to find their feminine energy and make it shine. It is based on a set of principles — receptiveness, politeness/grace, self-care, community, intuition, attraction and persuasion[22] — that are opposed to masculine energy, which is defined as projective, active, giving, expensive and outward.[23] Those influencers recognise that a woman can have both masculine and feminine energy. However, it is obvious that a woman's energy ought to be mostly feminine, and a man's mostly masculine. In fact, I couldn't find a single tutorial online on how to develop my masculine energy as a woman. On the contrary, content on how to develop a masculine energy as a man, or to get rid of one's masculine energy as a woman, were recommended to me.

Using essence and energies conveniently circumvents the controversial topic of biological differences which are used to legitimise gender roles. Implying that the feminine and the masculine are contrasting energies means that gender roles are a natural expression of those energies. Divine femininity influencers operate directly in female online spheres to restore feminine values. They create a safe space that nurtures sorority, just like feminist groups have historically done. In a way, divine femininity relates to what Professor Alice Echols named "cultural feminism", a branch that grew out of radical feminism in the late 1970s in the US. Cultural feminists aimed to create a female counterculture where male values would be exorcised and female values nurtured.[24] For instance, in the context of the climate crisis, essentialist (cultural) feminists have turned ecology into an extension of womanhood, understood as the capacity to create life. From it, they drew several values — care, receptiveness — that our culture needs to adopt in the fight against climate change. Essentialists believe that in order to restore a state of balance among all forms of life, one has to align themselves with the natural laws of the universe. Divine femininity is one of the ways through which women can achieve this.

However, the belief that society should be governed according to the natural laws of the universe is inadequate. There is an increasing gap between the way essentialists imagine the repartition of roles in society and how individuals choose to live their lives. French streamer @Cass_Andre looked at the typical life of a twenty-first-century Western woman and concluded that the act of procreation, as well as the feminine values assigned to it, cannot define the role of women in society, since most women only give birth once or twice in their entire lives, an increasing number do not want to have children, and some simply cannot have any due to infertility. Rather, a woman understands her place in the world in the way she is socialised from birth: when she is separated from boys, when she encounters sexism, when she is catcalled in the street. These are elements of a woman's daily life that signal to her that she is perceived as a woman.[25]

I'm reminded as I'm writing this of something French actor Omar Sy (who is known internationally for his role in the Netflix TV series *Lupin*) once said as he was promoting a film about Senegalese soldiers who fought with France during the First World War. He spoke about the administrative difficulties those soldiers faced when they applied for French citizenship and jokingly concluded that "those soldiers are in fact French, that's what being French means — having to deal with the nightmare that is the French administration".[26] Being a French person is more than a skin colour, a bloodline, it's something that is *felt* through specific experiences that all French people can relate to beyond their genetic differences.

Unsurprisingly, the divine femininity trend has found success among Black female audiences. I write unsurprisingly because Black femininity has been subjected to racist stereotypes for centuries. The hyper-sexualised jezebel, the rude and loud sapphire, or the unattractive mammy are some of them.[27] With divine femininity, many Black women have found a space in which they can define themselves as they please and explore femininity on their own terms.

When I was researching for my master's thesis three years ago, I came across the story of African American teacher Maryrose Reeves Allen. She was part of a movement that emerged at the beginning of the twentieth century which sought to turn respectability into a tool for the emancipation of Black people. From then on, African American leaders turned Black schools and universities into spaces of experimentation. Developing the aesthetic of the body became part of the education of students. In 1925, twenty-five-year-old Maryrose Reeves Allen joined the historically Black Howard University as a physical education teacher for girls.[28] She thought to elevate them by focusing on what she called the great *triumvirat*: body-mind-spirit.[29] She was opposed to superficial forms of beauty and preferred the formation of elegant bodies and minds through exercise. Her program consisted of a completely new approach to training in which femininity and charm cohabited with former imperatives of strength and health. Allen wanted to redefine beauty standards for Black women, as she noticed that people of colour tended to erase their unique identity in an attempt to fit with Hollywood's white beauty standards. Unfortunately, her project remained unclear and appeared to have some eugenic undertones.[30] Ultimately, Allen's body-mind-spirit approach to beauty wasn't sufficient to challenge deeply engrained racist beauty standards.

In many ways, today's Black divine femininity echoes Allen's project and its limits. Despite being described as a spiritual experience, video essayist Tee Noir noticed that Black women tend to understand divine femininity as an aesthetic, a way of *looking* very feminine.[31] Across social media platforms, Black divine femininity influencers explain to their audience how to become soft, how to get rid of their masculine energy by wearing feminine clothes, adopting a light, bright make-up, by smiling more, etc. They direct them towards role models like Lori Harvey, who fulfils all the divine femininity principles (receptiveness, politeness/grace, self-care, community, intuition, attraction and persuasion) — a "feminine hero", said Tee Noir. The aesthetic component of the trend is made clear when one compares the way people talk about Lori Harvey to other, less conventionally attractive Black women who nonetheless follow the same divine principles. Tee Noir used the example of Simone Biles, someone who "flips in the air for a living, and then lands gracefully on her feet, all while wearing a full face of makeup and a sparkly leotard". The only difference between Harvey and Biles is their physical appearance. Lori Harvey is closer to white, Western beauty standards than Simone Biles, and she is therefore perceived as more feminine.

The term "colourism" conceptualises the disparities in the way these two women are treated. Believed to have been coined by Pulitzer Prize winner Alice Walker, it refers to the "prejudicial or preferential treatment of same-race people based solely on their colour".[32] Social media has popularised the term using examples one can find in celebrity culture.[33] Lori Harvey, Rihanna, Regé-Jean Page and Zendaya might face racial discrimination, just like Lupita Nyong'o, Daniel Kaluuya or Simone Biles. However, the facial features and skin colour of the first group are closer to white, Western beauty standards when compared to the second, which is something that can benefit them in a society that continues to value whiteness over darker skin colours. That is why Black activists and scholars demand that efforts towards the equality of opportunity and better representation include an understanding of the specificity of colourism.[34]

It seems that in the quest to become traditionally feminine, women of colour are pushed to reject everything that is unique to their ethnicity and comply with the aesthetic and culture of white people. For many Black women, being traditionally feminine is not a lifestyle choice, but a necessity given the way society treats them. In one of her videos, video essayist Amanda Maryanna looked at a large selection of contemporary romcoms and asked: "Why can't black women be the love interest?" She was specifically interested in the TV series *Modern Love*, inspired by the *New York Times* column of the same name, which showcases various stories of love, betrayal and sex. As a young Black woman, Amanda searched for an episode with a Black female love interest and, guess what? She couldn't find any.[35] The lack of Black female representation in *Modern Love* (set in one of the most diverse cities on Earth) is far from being an anomaly. In the comments section under the video, a Black female viewer also complained that when Black women finally get to become the love interest, it seems that they must go through traumatic events or face racial injustice to gain value in the viewer's eye. Black women understand that their existence as human beings isn't enough to deserve love.

In one of the episodes of the podcast *Fresh and Fit*, co-host Myron Gaines got annoyed that people called him racist for not wanting to date Black women. "I'm not racist, it's a preference".[36] Is it though? In a study on US intermarriage rates conducted in 2013, sociologist Wendy Wang showed that while a quarter of Black men intermarry, less than one in eight Black women do. On the contrary, a third of Asian women intermarry, and only one in six Asian men do. White people don't intermarry much, less than one in thirteen.[37] Love isn't colour-blind. Preferences aren't just preferences. The study clearly underlines unequal gender and racial dynamics between heterosexual men and women in intermarriage. Stereotypically "innocent and feminine" Asian women intermarry more than "aggressive and masculine" Black women, and a significant portion of Black men and Asian women find a spouse outside their race group.[38] What the study points to is how race plays into the politics of desirability. Being desirable to the eyes of others means being marriage material, attractive, or simply "fuckable".[39] As the data shows, certain combinations of gender and race are deemed less desirable than others and that has consequences on an individual's sense of self-worth.

In one of the episodes of her *Lovers and Friends* podcast, intimacy expert and sexologist Shan Boodram invited on actor and comedian Jasmin Brown. The episode was titled "I Baby My Man and It Works for Us". Brown describes herself as a submissive partner to an alpha man. She cooks for her man, she does the laundry for him, she packs his bags, she makes sure he sleeps well, she treats him like a mother would treat her child, and more importantly, she finds joy in doing that. The episode sparked a lot of discussion on social media. Some defended Jasmin, arguing that she was not submissive, that she served him but remained autonomous. Others heavily criticised her for acting like a mother and not asking anything in return. As Jasmin herself said, she studies her man, she has an A+ in his studies, but had to think for a few seconds when Shan asked her if he had an A+ in her studies — "I think so..." she hesitantly answered. In the responses to her story, many Black commentators linked Jasmin's submission to the social implications of being a Black woman. They regretted that even a successful and conventionally attractive divine woman like Jasmin had to lower her standards to the bare minimum.[40] The imperatives of traditional femininity, camouflaged as divine femininity, become more severe for those that society does not deem desirable.

Before we conclude this section, I would like to use Jasmin Brown's story to delve a bit more into the concept of choice feminism. Like the tradwives we mentioned earlier, Jasmin looked very satisfied with her life and claimed it is her choice to live that way. She asserted her subjectivity in the act of choosing to be submissive to her boyfriend. Such a statement sounds contradictory to me, and maybe to you as well. It is tempting at this moment to want to reject choice feminism because there is nothing feminist about choosing to be submissive, it has gone too far. It is also at the precise moment when judgemental thoughts foment that one has to pause and reflect. Accepting the fact that we might not understand someone's life experience is proof of humility. It is important to grasp that each woman is on her own path and that no one has the authority to establish what is the correct one. So instead of imposing one's vision of feminism onto others, we can first listen, maybe ask questions, and start a conversation.

Shan Boodram beautifully handled her conversation with Jasmin. As a Black woman herself, she was able to connect with her guest on a level that I, as a white woman, simply cannot. She accepted her the way she is and asked questions to challenge her in a compassionate way. In other words, she respected Jasmin's choice, but refused to end the conversation there. She avoided confrontation, because doing so can foster reactance, and, in all honesty, we cannot afford to alienate women like Jasmin from the feminist cause. Starting from the basis that a woman's choice ought to be respected, the interlocutor can then navigate difficult yet necessary conversations with the certainty that no one's acting superior to the other.

That is also what content creator Breeny Lee did when she turned Jasmin's story into an opportunity to discuss a Black woman's place in relation to her man and society. The premise of Black sorority allowed her to constructively criticise Jasmin and other Black women who choose to submit to their husbands or boyfriends. The controversiality of the topic was naturally well handled by someone who could relate to Jasmin's intersectional experience. As a Black Christian herself, Breeny Lee understood where Jasmin was coming from, but told Black women to see their value, increase their standards, and add "tax and inflation cause times are hard!"[41] Tee Noir also expanded on the topic of Black women's submission to their boyfriends or husbands by showing how the intersection of misogyny, racism and colourism impacts the woman's ability to honestly choose for herself. Those conversations felt productive and relevant to Black feminism and, by extension, the entire feminist movement.

The beauty of intersectional feminism is its plurality. It has the ambition to accommodate individuals of various backgrounds and will not compromise on it. It understands the feminist experience not as a recipe but as a vehicle, a continuous stream in which individuals across the gender spectrum hop in at various stages of their lives to be carried into a never-ending exploration of themselves and the world. In-group discussions are the solution to the limits of choice feminism — meaning its tendency to depoliticise the personal — precisely because they investigate the personal from a place of understanding. Within their communities, women forge ideas that — once they expand beyond the community's boundaries — make the movement more powerful. It is a horizontal approach to feminism where community bubbles co-exist within a larger feminist movement. That movement does not belong to anybody, there is no hierarchy. However, it relies on communities' capacity to simultaneously valorise their specificity and accept a certain degree of intermixing.[42]

Conservative women rigorously refuse any form of intermixing. They use and abuse choice feminism in a way that *strictly* closes the door to the politicisation of their personal choices, since doing the contrary would force them to expose their own political agenda.

From Conservative Lifestyle to Conservative Politics

In the comments section of one of tradwife Alena Kate Pettitt's videos, a viewer warned her to "be careful when using the term tradwife. It is associated with white supremacy." To which she replied:

> Thank you for making me aware of that — something that is clearly not in my vocabulary, and I'm shocked actually. Such a shame that something meant to describe a wholesome, vintage dynamic should be used to promote racism... What a world we live in.[43]

I find that reply to be particularly amusing given the comments Alena had made in a BBC video story on her. In fact, when asked about how Britishness fits into the tradwife lifestyle, she answered — sitting at a table in front of freshly bought flowers positioned in a way that slightly covered a framed picture of the British flag with the slogan "TRULY GREAT" — that it was important to her. "Times are changing so fast and we don't even know the identity of our country right now", she said.[44] The concept of Britishness was first introduced to me during an English class at *le lycée* (the French equivalent for year 11 to 13 in the UK and high school in the US). We were told by our teacher that it refers to all the things that make a person feel British. Embracing Britishness was even a requirement to become a British citizen, we were told. That is why anyone who seeks to remain indefinitely in the UK must pass the Life in the United Kingdom test. The structure and content of the test help us to understand what is truly hidden behind the term "Britishness". It refers to a specific language, a national history, but also a specific skin colour, ethnicity and religion. That is why British journalist Afua Hirsch titled her book on the topic *Brit(ish)*, therefore reflecting her struggle to identify with Britishness as it is currently defined. Hirsch was heavily criticised for pointing a finger at a reality that many refuse to see. She was too demanding, ungrateful and unpatriotic.

On the contrary, patriotic Alena Kate Pettitt described herself as "selfless", "the opposite of that is someone who is inherently selfish and just takes".[45] Put back into context, she used this comparison to judge women who do not prioritise family life. By doing so, she set up herself as the target of online criticism, waves of dislikes and mockery she could then utilise to further advance her conservative cause. In one of her videos, commentator and video essayist Tara Mooknee showed how leftist critiques of tradwife content were recuperated by the conservative online ecosystem to paint the left as cruel.[46] In what she called a "coming-out" video, Abigail Shapiro Roth, sister of the famous political American commentator Ben Shapiro, proudly declared that she was a conservative influencer. She said that "so much of the time, it feels like one world view, one position is tolerated. And none of them will say what I am about to: I'm a conservative influencer."[47] The video is titled "Conservative Women, It's Our Time || Let's Take Our Culture Back", which is evocative of the rhetoric of both social movements and the culture wars.

Conservative feminism, as it is called by its advocates, gathers a variety of women. Some are primarily homemakers like Alena Kate Pettitt and Abigail Shapiro Roth, others are primarily girlbosses like Anna Bey and Ivanka Trump, who appears on her Twitter banner with her baby on her lap and a laptop in front of her. Kellyanne Conway, Trump's former Senior Counselor, who is known for having coined the phrase "alternative facts", said conservative feminism helps her look at herself "as a product of [her] choices, not a victim of [her] circumstances".[48] She used the example of her mum, who didn't rely on government support to get herself and her daughter Kellyanne out of a tricky situation — "she just figured it out".[49] The right-wing rhetoric of self-reliance is applied to conservative feminism through mothers' selflessness. In turn, mothers' selflessness becomes, in the eyes of conservatives, a political asset in their campaigns on self-reliance.

In 2008, Sarah Palin shared the Republican ticket as Vice President with presidential candidate John McCain. Coming from a small town in Alaska, Palin was known for being a "hockey mom". She built her campaign around the civic values of motherhood and continued to do so even after the ticket's defeat. In fact, during the following senatorial elections, she talked about being like a "mama grizzly" — she ended up meeting a real mama bear on a boat trip a year later, but that is another story.[50] Palin's strategy of staking her vice-presidential campaign on motherhood was not revolutionary in any way. The ideal of the "Republican Mother" already existed in the US in the eighteenth century, a time where middle-class American mothers were expected to transfer the values and ideals of Republicanism from one generation to the next. Their role was deeply valued by society but not emancipatory, since it did not liberate them from the domestic sphere. In other words, American women had a civic role, not a political one. It aligned with conservatives' belief that men and women are better off when they operate in separate spheres.[51] Later, in the nineteenth century, in connection with the temperance campaign, sections of the US Women's Suffrage Movement demanded the right to vote on the basis that women are the procreators and carers of the next generation of citizens, and therefore should have a say in political affairs. Cartoons of the time depicted men as corrupted and greedy, while women were portrayed as innocent, selfless and nurturing.

This strategy continues to be used today by women across the political spectrum. Motherhood is perceived as a sign of respectability, something that deserves to be put forward in a political campaign speech or in a social media bio. Ivanka Trump, Hillary Clinton and Elizabeth Warren all have the term "mother" or "mom" in the first line of their Twitter bios. Funnily enough, motherhood does not really influence electability,[52] so it is interesting to see that even Democrats continue to display it so predominantly or use it politically. It reveals how essentialism is entrenched in society and persists even when it does not have any reason to.

Before we proceed with the second part, I want to explore an example of a group of women who stepped out of patriarchal femininity. Unless one is encouraged to question those biases, one naturally operates according to them and therefore participates in naturalising them. What allowed me to challenge my own biases were both my life experience and the reading of feminist literature. Because of the latter, I often get told that I have unlearned certain biases to learn new ones, and that feminist literature doesn't deconstruct anything, it rather injects gender ideology into someone's head. While I fully disagree with such a statement, I also want to highlight that feminism is not the only way through which one can deconstruct gender. In fact, the process of deconstruction is not always conscious, verbalised — *it just happens.*

Fitgirls and Gender

As a passionate tennis player born in the late 1990s, I was inspired by two very distinct female role models: the tall, slim, green-eyed and pale-skinned Maria Sharapova, and the tall, muscular, brown-eyed and dark-skinned Serena Williams. As I closely followed these two women's performances, I couldn't help but notice how differently people talked about them. Maria Sharapova was elegant, sexy, she was known for grunting and became a sexual fantasy for a lot of men (there are countless video compilations of her grunting on YouTube, and many Instagram pages full of pictures of her with her skirt raised while serving…). On the other hand, every single time Serena played, someone around me, usually at my tennis club, would comment that "she didn't look very feminine", or say, "she's too muscular", "she's not my type", (well, good for you, because neither are you, fifty-year-old man). As someone who has always found muscular women particularly good-looking but has also internalised the fact that being too muscular equals not being attractive, I couldn't help but wonder at which specific moment one goes from sexy and elegant to "she's not my type".

Serena and Venus Williams have been subjected to a lot of criticism on their physique. Some people even "transinvestigated" them, meaning that they analysed pictures from their childhood and hypothesised that they were born male.[53] Muscle mass and womanhood aren't compatible, it seems. In fact, the fitness desirability standards for women consist in having toned abs, toned arms and legs, a firm, full booty and *nothing* more than that. Fitness coaches report that women often refuse to lift heavy weights because they are afraid to cross the line between toned and bulky. YouTube, one of the world's most popular websites, reflects those concerns. When you type "grow glutes with" in the search bar, the most popular search results appear in a list. Among them are "grow glutes without legs", "grow glutes without weights", "grow glutes without squats", "grow glutes without thighs". In just a few clicks, you end up on tutorials scoring millions of views and explaining "How to Grow Your Butt WITHOUT Growing Your Thighs" (ten million views), "20 MIN. BUTT LIFT WORKOUT on the floor - grow butt without thighs / NO SQUATS NO JUMPS" (4.1 million views). Likewise, videos explaining how to "SHRINK YOUR WAIST" or "AVOID MAKING YOUR WAIST THICK" get just as much attention. Fitness superstars like Cassey Ho from *Blogilates* or Karena and Katrina from *ToneItUp* offer millions of women a version of fitness that is compatible with traditional femininity.

As I have already mentioned, fitness is part of the routine of the ideal woman. The way women conventionally train has not changed in the last centuries. They started doing sports as soon as their male counterparts — around the second half of the nineteenth century in France and a little bit earlier in the UK. While men's sports quickly diversified and branched out into unions and federations, women's sports remained limited. Sources show that women were trained in archery, running, fencing, ice skating, tennis and gymnastics, but those practices had to remain moderate, discreet and aesthetically pleasing.[54] A woman's fitness was a sign that she would give birth and raise healthy and strong individuals. On the other hand, sports should not interfere with the duties of motherhood, or the imperatives of femininity.[55]

In 1917, French sportswoman Alice Milliat challenged male-led sports institutions by creating the *Fédération Française*

Sportive Féminine (the French Female Sports Federation).[56] Thanks to her dedication, the first international women's sports event, the Women's Olympiad, was organised five years later. At the 1928 Olympics, twenty-five-year-old Lina Radke won the first ever women's 800m final, and in doing established the first world record (which lasted until 1944), but the quality of the race didn't make it into the newspapers' headlines. Instead, the state of exhaustion and fatigue of the women after the race became the centre of attention. Wrong impressions and falsified reports concluded that women were too delicate and physically incapable of doing such sports. As a result, the event was removed from the Games for the next thirty-two years.[57] Still today, a double standard persists. For instance, female rugby players are not perceived the same way as artistic swimmers. Their muscle mass and bulky physique is a threat. The media systematically frame their masculinity as something negative. Because of that, many female athletes choose to over-perform femininity with colourful long hair, long nails, makeup, jewellery, etc.[58]

Today's fitgirl influencers perform femininity in and outside the gym in the same way female athletes do. Most of them discovered fitness through workout-at-home tutorials but weren't satisfied with them. To be honest, you cannot grow a booty without heavy weights, squats, deadlifts and hip thrusts. And where can those weights and machines be found? At the gym! Former lifestyle influencers or newly born fitgirls started showing themselves going to the gym, sharing their intense workout routines, and how they use the equipment in vlogs. By doing so, they demystified the gym and motivated a generation of young women to join them on their journey. The brand Gymshark grew out of a garage in Birmingham and blew up on YouTube by partnering with emerging fitness influencers. It created gym wear (in collaboration with its fitgirl ambassadors) that was designed to truly make women feel good and comfortable. Leggings became squat-proof, the designs looked cute, the shape and details enhanced one's body type. Women started wearing the brand in and outside of the gym, turning their sports activity into a lifestyle. Progressively, lifting weights also became less of a taboo. Women who went to the gym enjoyed the feeling of strength, the soreness, the exhaustion of a good workout.

Popular influencers like Whitney Simmons or Natacha Océane have shared how they used to work out to achieve the smallest figure possible and changed their mindset around health and fitness throughout the years thanks to bodybuilding and strength training.[59] French fitgirl @Jujufitcat described her journey from calorie-burning home workouts to CrossFit as "therapy".[60] Video transformations of women going from calorie-restricting skinny to muscular have become popular. They are inspirational because they show how increasing one's muscle mass not only makes you look and feel stronger, but also increases your metabolism, which means you don't have to restrict your calories if you want to remain slim. The health benefits of lifting weights (both physical and psychological), the lifestyle, the energy you get from being more active continuously convince women to give up on preconceived norms of femininity, to make them pointless. The way fitgirls play with gender expression is fascinating to me. Like Serena Williams, fitgirls bring fashion to sports. Outside the gym or the tennis court, they highlight their strong physique with close-fitting, feminine clothing. By surpassing the expectation of women to remain soft, innocent and weak, these women open the door for a broader deconstruction of gender norms.

Three years ago, BS PhD and fitness influencer Stephanie

Buttermore went on an all-in journey after developing unhealthy diet habits. Going all-in meant that she would eat as much as she wanted for a year, no restriction, no limit. Naturally, her body got larger as the months passed by to the point where she had gained forty pounds (eighteen kilos). In an explanatory video, Stephanie shared her desire to leave aesthetics to the side to work on her health.[61] She was willing to experience the weight gain and the fatphobia that would come with it. In a similar way, MMA champion Tévy Say had to face her female friends' concerns as she started getting muscular. She would tell them that she was passionate about MMA and in order to get better at it, she had to build a decent muscle mass.[62] That's it.

Putting performance or health before aesthetics as a woman is subversive. It challenges the politics of desirability by expanding the definition of what someone who identifies as a woman looks like, or more precisely, what being a woman comfortable in her body looks like. It's the comfort from which these women challenge those norms that makes it so radical. They are not motivated by "gender ideology", most of them probably wouldn't identify as feminists, but their experience with sports is just as emancipatory.

In activist and online political spheres, what these women do is coherent with a greater movement towards body neutrality. Body neutrality refuses to attach a moral judgement, whether positive (body positivity) or negative (fatphobia, gender discrimination) to any body. It sounds like a new concept, but has already existed in many countries for a very long time. It opens the doors to a world where gender norms are an afterthought. It leads the way to a post-gender society where women's nipples can be free without being sexualised (and removed from Instagram), where body hairs are not a sign of a lack of hygiene, where femininity and masculinity aren't gatekept by women for the former and men for the latter. It simply makes sure everybody can experiment with gender, find what makes them feel comfortable, and have fun. However, such a project is met with great resistance.

Already in the 1960s, women athletes whose physique and performance were outstanding were assigned a femininity test.[63] Recently, Caster Semenya, a South-African runner, was accused by many — including her female competitors — of being a man disguised as a woman. Semenya is a hyperandrogenic woman, which means she produces an abnormal amount of testosterone. Nevertheless, her personal records do not reach the minimum required for male competitions. She remains a woman and ought to compete in women's competitions. With the rise of the internet, anybody can publicly speculate on "gender inversions". This practice now has a name: "transinvestigation". As I mentioned previously, the Williams sisters have been subjected to it since their childhood. Michelle Obama, Angelina Jolie, Sandra Bullock, Melania Trump, Kate Middleton, Sarah Palin, Marilyn Monroe, Grace Jones and many other (mostly) women are also suspected of "gender inversion". A square jaw, square shoulders, narrow hips, a flat chin, a seemingly appearing Adam's apple are "male biological markers" that investigators look for.

However, transinvestigators' urge to speculate on every single celebrity that does not have all the right "biological gender markers" is quite comical and profoundly counterproductive. In fact, the accumulation of gender "irregularities" only serves to prove that gender expression cannot be constrained to a strict binary since most people do not rigorously fit in either category.[64] Even Ben Shapiro, who worries about the feminisation of men and what he calls "transgenderism", does not look or sound very masculine, and it's fine. Gender is a spectrum. Even sex is a spectrum. Every year, it is estimated that 1.7% of new-borns are intersex, meaning that they have several sex characteristics that "do not fit typical binary notions of male or female bodies".[65] As a woman with PCOS (polycystic ovary syndrome), a condition that affects around 10% of people who menstruate, I've had to deal with an abnormal level of testosterone that has had consequences on my body, that made me feel less feminine and ultimately challenged my vision of what being a woman means. The cult of the gender/sex binary is frankly exhausting and harmful. It leads intersex and trans people to go through long and costly gender-affirming surgeries to "cure" a "biological anomaly" for the first group or "gender dysphoria" for the second.

In an article for *Trans Writes*, YouTuber and actress Abigail Thorn argued that we have completely got it wrong with dysphoria, that trans people aren't the only ones to experience gender dysphoria, cis people — to a lesser degree — also do.[66] In fact, when a woman spends thousands of dollars on breast implants or laser hair removal, when a young man prays every morning in front of the mirror for facial hair and muscles to finally grow, isn't it gender dysphoria, too?[67] Yes!, Thorn answers. But if it is that common, then why is it only used when talking about trans people? Why does such a concept even exist? Because it serves to frame those who experience it as deviant and adds a hurdle to accessing medical care. On the other hand, those who seek to further affirm their gender assigned at birth through surgery (a cis woman getting ribs removed or a cis man getting jaw fillers) do not necessarily need a psychological diagnosis.

Part II: A Failed Sexual Revolution?

Today's debates and discussions around sexual liberation imply that it was a failure in many ways. The criticism coming from the right is unsurprisingly not nuanced. The rise and politicisation of the manosphere, as well as the plethora of content targeting hook-up culture, dating apps and unconventional forms of relationships, are symptomatic of a backlash. In left-wing circles, the criticism of sexual liberation is related to anti-capitalist sentiments. Specifically, it is argued that consumerism has penetrated our love lives. Another critique, a feminist one, argues that women did not enjoy the benefits of sexual liberation as much as men, especially "high status men". In this second part, we will look at the different ways in which anti-sexual-liberation rhetoric is articulated and how it spreads in online communities.

While for many scholars the sexual revolution started way before the 1960s, that decade is remembered by the public as a turning point in the history of feminism. The 1960s-1970s sexual revolution was marked by the greater acceptance of sex outside the traditional heterosexual married couple. Feminist organisations like NOW and LGBT movements like the Gay Liberation Front participated in normalising the use of contraception and the legalisation of abortion, homosexuality, premarital sex, masturbation, pornography, etc. Conservatives saw in this revolution the rise of the "permissive society" they still criticise today. Progressives, on the other hand, sought to break away from strict morals that prevented the individual from exploring their sexuality in all its forms. The fight for reproductive rights culminated in France in 1975, with the Veil law. Together with the support and pressure of feminist organisations, former minister of health Simone Veil and the French government decriminalised abortion. Two years beforehand, the US Supreme Court ruled that the constitution conferred the right to abortion in the landmark *Roe v. Wade* decision that was overturned in 2022. The revolution also encouraged progress in scientific research. Greater attention was given to women's health and sex education.

Five years after #MeToo, the notion of consent has come to dominate public discussions on sex and intimacy. In August 2022, Spain passed the "only yes means yes" sexual consent law.[1] Schools and universities have launched programs to educate the youth on consent and implemented regulations to sanction acts of misconduct. Teenagers are now expected to memorise the consent rules, so please repeat after me: "no means no — only yes means yes — your partner can change their mind during the intercourse". Even pick-up artists, known in feminist spheres for promoting street harassment and sexual assault, upgraded to the post-#MeToo era. In *Men Who Hate Women*, Laura Bates writes about pick-up artist Owen Cook, who used to advocate physically grabbing women in public and practising first on unattractive women to overcome their "this-is-not-the-behaviour-I'm-supposed-to-be-doing-block". In his videos following #MeToo, Cook instead brags about teaching men "how to approach girls respectfully without creeping them out", audaciously lamenting the fact that "women are often BOTHERED in the street by men who are unable to read their signals!"[2]

Hundreds of self-help articles, podcasts and videos have capitalised on the notion of consent or (a less heavily connoted phrase) "setting boundaries". Self-proclaimed experts recommend that women "own [their] power to bring him closer",[3] they warn them that "a lack of boundaries invites a lack of respect". Women "need to be able to tell people no", they "need to be able to let people know when [it's] going too far", they "have to draw the line".[4] In *Tomorrow Sex Will Be Good Again*, Katherine Angel argues that what she calls "consent culture" operates exactly like confidence culture:

> Consent [...] places the burden of good sexual interaction on women's behaviour — on what they want and on what they can know and say about their wants; on their ability to perform a confident sexual self in order to ensure that sex is mutually pleasurable and non-coercive.[5]

The dating app Bumble, founded in 2014 by Tinder co-founder Whitney Wolfe Herd, is a good example of what Angel describes. Herd claims that everything they do at Bumble "is driven by female empowerment".[6] On the app, women send a message first, they have control. Men cannot access them without their confident approval. But all that so-called female empowerment is limited to the initial text. Bumble only disrupts one aspect of what philosopher Amia Srinivasan described as the "informal regulatory system of gendered sexual expectations".[7] In it can be regrouped things like "women who sexually excite men are supposed to finish the job", or "going home from the bar alone [without a girl] makes you a loser".[8] Taking into account those gendered sexual expectations means that we have to complexify our understanding of consent. In fact, the belief that enthusiastic consent is the key to solve the problem of sexual violence is flawed, for how do you know when you don't know?[9] Well, Srinivasan would probably argue that most women answer by following gendered sexual expectations. Because of that, women can retrospectively feel violated for having done things they did not want to do but felt they had to. That frustration and sometimes anger is turned towards themselves, for not being confident enough to set boundaries like that relationships expert on YouTube told you to, and also towards the sex partner who does not have to care about any of that and who ultimately benefits from those gendered expectations.

In a response video to a series of allegations of sexual assault and misconduct, YouTube star Andrew Callaghan recognised that his understanding of consent was flawed and that, despite allegedly respecting women's *no*, his tendency to make unwanted advances, of having a hard time with rejection, could pressure women into consenting to have sexual interactions with him.[10] On the other hand, women can feel pressured to appear as "the cool girl", a phrase that was first popularised by the film *Gone Girl*. In it, main character Amy goes on a bitter monologue explaining that "cool girl is hot, cool girl is gang, cool girl is fun, cool girl never gets angry at her man, she only smiles in a chagrined loving manner, and then presents her mouth for fucking". The segment was clipped out of the film and circulated online. In an Instagram post that went viral, @_mia_india_ used the phrase to describe what men mean when they say they want a cool girl: (1) a girl without the confidence to set boundaries; (2) a girl that "goes with the flow"... meaning is passive to whatever HE wants to do; (3) a girl that won't rightfully protest when he has mistreated her; and (4) a girl that doesn't align with feminist communities and "just gets on so much better with guys than other girls".[11] The amount of likes and shares on this particular post is proof of how relatable the "cool girl" is to women.

The debates on consent and gendered sexual expectations that emerged post-#MeToo branched out in two directions. Some feminists like Angel and Srinivasan advocated for a progressive outcome — one that is decentralised from consent and includes the notion of desire. Their work has trickled down to online feminist circles but has struggled to expand beyond them. Another branch of feminists has instead pivoted in another, more conservative direction. They agree that consent does not necessarily translate into a safe, satisfying sexual life for women. However, they say that feminists lied to women when they told them that sexual activity is liberating. Instead, they promote a sort of "common sense" feminism that simultaneously celebrates the advances made by the long feminist movement and romanticises a more conservative past. Connected to this new wave of feminists, Franco-Israeli sociologist Eva Illouz argues that sexual freedom, in the form of casual sex, open relationships and flaky marriages (what she called negative relationships), has become the neoliberal philosophy of the private sphere.[12] She concludes her book titled *The End of Love* by quoting Irving Howe's argument that "the defence of a return to the 'conservative' institution of the family becomes, under totalitarianism, a subversive act"[13], a quote she relates to the omnipresence of capitalism in our lives. Even though she claims that her work does not encourage a return to family values, it is hard to sincerely believe her, given how, like Howe, she romanticises the family as a locus for resistance, and, throughout her book, laments its disintegration by the forces of capitalism.

The premise of Illouz's criticism can hardly be contested. It is undeniable that hook-up culture, including dating apps, has a bad reputation. I have personally never met anyone who has spoken enthusiastically about them. On social media, content on the toxicity of dating apps get a lot of engagement because of how consensual this point of view is. Everybody, from left-wing social commentators to mega influencers like Jordan B. Peterson or Russell Band, complains about them, and it is precisely from this place of consensus that social conservatives like Illouz develop their critique of sexual liberation. *The End of Love* offers a collection of examples for us to understand how it happens, namely how the anti-sexual-liberation rhetoric is forged. My goal is not to point at Illouz in particular but rather to highlight patterns that are recognisable in conservative online discourse. So here we go.

In her part on casual sex, Illouz uses the example of men at parties who stick their genitals in the back of a woman to signal they want to have sex. It allows her to define casual sex as a "symbolic strateg[y] to de-singularize the sexual partner". By doing so, she implies that the assumption of a casual sex friendly environment makes men feel it is legitimate to sexually harass women. In fact, parties are one setting in which men *believe* they have sexual access to women regardless of their consent. The home, the school, the workplace, the street and public transportation are other environments where such things occur. The problem is not casual sex, like Illouz seems to suggest. There was no pre-casual-sex world in which every single man was a gentleman and women did not get sexually assaulted or harassed.

Later in the book, Illouz (I) shares a segment of an interview she conducted with a woman (V):

I: Can you describe to me how a typical interaction on Tinder would go?

V: So you go through the profiles. Most of them, you don't like their face. It's actually fun to swipe left. It's very nice to do that to the faces of men who look macho, arrogant, or dumb.

I: But some you like?

V: Sure.

I: What happens then?

V: You swipe right, and if they've swiped right as well, we start chatting, exchanging text. Usually the conversation gets quickly sexual.

I: How for example? Do you feel comfortable telling me?

V: Oh sure! It goes like this: "Hi. Do you want to meet?" "Yes. I'd like that." "Tell me what you're thinking about?" You would typically answer something sexual. "I am getting hot here. I can meet you in ten minutes at [name of a bar]. I am getting really hot here." You can also add, if you want to really turn them on: "I think I'm gonna suck you hard."

I: You say this is a normal, regular way of interacting before meeting?

V: Yes. Totally normal. No one thinks there is anything unusual about it. I mean, that's why you got in touch with him in the first place.

As someone who has spent a decent amount of time on dating apps matching with men, I don't agree with V that this interaction is normal. However, I cannot solely draw conclusions from my own experience, so I asked my Instagram followers. Most of them are between the age of eighteen to thirty, with an almost 50/50 split between men/women ratio, and some non-binary people. I was immediately reassured. Among the 923 replies I received, 87% of them said V's experience on Tinder isn't typical.[14] Some told me they have had weird, impersonal experiences on Tinder, but that this one sounded very unsafe and unnatural. In this case, as well as in the previous one, Illouz uses extreme anecdotes that help her caricature casual sex into something inherently toxic. She makes it impossible to envision care and reciprocity as "people engaging in casual sex *must* remain strangers to each other".[15] Nothing better exemplifies Illouz's point than "dick pics". Unsurprisingly, the author reduces them to yet another by-product of sexual liberation, forgetting that men have been masturbating in front of women without their consent for a very long time.[16]

Casual sex is one of many phenomena that mirror everything that is wrong with how we do relationships. It is not the origin of the problem but rather a medium. By focusing on the medium, one avoids addressing the elephant(s) in the room: sexual violence and sexual expectations. In other words, if casual sex is inherently toxic, there is no hope to reform it, all that can be done is restrict it. Such a lazy approach prevents us from imagining a practice of casual sex that does preserve care and reciprocity. In fact, earlier in the book, Illouz describes a sexual encounter between three people at a party in which consent was respected and in which each participant was taken care of and got an equally pleasurable experience. The fact that she still attached a negative connotation to her description made me realise that it is precisely the unconventional, liberated character of casual sex that truly bothers social conservatives like her.

Casual sex can be based on friendships in which participants value the other individual not because they possess each other, but because they truly care about giving and receiving pleasure. I particularly resonated with something Maddie Dragsbaek said in a podcast episode on the topic:

> You can be non-committed and also give a fuck about each other, and I hate that caring, and giving a shit about each other, and holding space emotionally for people before, during, and after sex is seen as too much of an investment.[17]

I asked my followers to share with me positive casual sex experiences and here is an answer I found heart-warming:

<u>Female, 18-24 years old, France, Paris</u>

I was in a period of my life where I only dated for fun in the hope of forgetting my ex. I found a guy on Tinder who had a scooter and I asked him to take me on a ride. The first date went super well, I got my scooter ride in Paris like in those very cliché movies. And beyond the "just for fun, nothing serious" we immediately bonded. Spontaneous conversations, strong attraction. I had bonded with a lot of guys like that, very intensely, from the first date, but it usually didn't go anywhere. That time it did. We weren't looking for something serious, our temperaments were completely different, the cliché of opposites attract, but in the matter of six months, we ended up bringing so much for each other. Our relationship was very special, today we could call it "situationship" since we knew from the beginning that he was going to move abroad, and I was going to study in another city. But I had the chance to meet someone who cured me from a painful break-up, with whom I shared deep intimacy, really good times, meaningful conversations. Without necessarily the intensity and commitment that requires a romantic relationship, something that was not possible for the both of us at that time in our lives, we evolved together with our lows and our differences. It wasn't easy due to attachment, but we stay in touch and remember it fondly ☺.

Others shared how dating apps allowed them to find friends and more, explore their sexuality, learn about new tricks and become more comfortable with their bodies.[18] As Maddie Dragsbaek said, dating apps are still very new and we are in the process of understanding how to navigate them on both an individual and collective level.

Another element of Illouz's analysis that is characteristic of the anti-sexual-liberation rhetoric is her focus on young single men. She highlights the absence of a clear script and rituals that make young single men feel lost. Through Durkheim's writings, Illouz compares them to the married man, who has a vision of the future and is guaranteed, through the institution of marriage, the continued possession of pleasures.[19] In fact, the idea that men only start to behave when they enter a relationship is widespread. The commitment to a woman through an official relationship or marriage (so through God and/or the State) is supposed to mark a shift from frivolous young adulthood to real manhood. That is why the delay of the age of marriage and the rise of less conventional forms of relationships have become a source of societal concern. If stable, committed relationships and marriage aren't as natural, what will discipline men? In *The End of Love*, Illouz tells the story of a nineteen-year-old man dating a fifteen-year-old girl. The man was into video games, he didn't put a lot of effort into the relationship, he didn't want to have sex, he said that he took her for granted because he was comfortable with the relationship, but still "f[ought] for her to stay".[20] Their relationship oscillated between open and exclusive according to the man's wants until she found another boyfriend who was her age and with whom she was willing to commit to an exclusive relationship. The flexible structure of the relationship, the absence of a script, is presented by the author as the reason why it failed. The fact that the girl (fifteen) might have felt deeply unsatisfied by the relationship and under pressure to remain close to him (who was nineteen) is not even considered.

The same analysis is reproduced in the chapter on divorce. Illouz separates "objective" divorce from "more abstract and affective" divorce (also called "no-fault" divorces). She concludes that the second category of divorces is often the result of "individual temperament",[21] and epiphanies of loving and unloving. There is no need to say that Illouz's comments on emotional break-ups and divorce sound very paternalistic. They imply that people don't take marriage seriously and loosely care about the psychological repercussions of separation. Those comments must also be put into context. Specifically, women are more likely to leave and men to suffer from it.[22] Her message therefore primarily targets heterosexual women. She focuses on the pain ("selfish") decisions can cause, as well as men's difficulty in properly taking care of themselves in the aftermath of such an event. The idea that separation can be a positive thing is not really considered. The long-term benefits of the liberation from an unsatisfactory relationship are overshadowed by the damage it temporarily causes.

To add more context, women are more likely to seek therapy or counselling for the management of their emotional self and relationships.[23] Boyfriends and husbands benefit from it in the form of second-hand therapy. It is therefore legitimate for a woman to want to devote more time and energy to herself, her hobbies, friendships, or to a partner who is willing to work on themselves and the relationship.

Social conservatives' solution to the end of love, namely the end of traditional, contractual forms of love, is nostalgia. In their ideal world, men and women live happily ever after. The man suddenly abandons his carelessness through his commitment to a woman for life. The woman oversees the fulfilment of her husband's emotional and sexual needs — she is the one in charge of disciplining him. But like in Disney movies, the female side of the relationship isn't shown, they lived happily ever after and *that's it*. We'll never know if Ariel, Cinderella, Jasmine, or Aurora truly lived happily ever after, as artist Saint Hoax highlighted in his awareness campaign for domestic violence, where he represented those princesses as bruised and bloodied. That is not part of the script.

Sociologist Melinda Cooper sees in Eva Illouz the rise of a new wave of left-wing social conservatives who deplore that the flexibility of work was met with a "flexible family" structure.[24] Members of this group tend to blame the counterculture, the artistic left of the 1960s, and the feminist movement that came with it for the disruption of post-war socialist ideals that preserved the family unit. Such a critique then allows them to frame the family as a subversive force that can resist the disintegration of social structures.[25] However, Cooper argues that this section of the left has wrongly reduced capitalism to economic liberalism. Instead, she writes that capitalism is constituted of a double movement of "preservation through transformation".[26] The first part (neoliberalism) serves to transform, to deregulate and to disintegrate for competitiveness; while the second part (conservatism) seeks to repair and to preserve so that wealth is passed from one generation to the next. The institution of the family is essential to the existence of capitalism. Cooper therefore demands that we resist the temptation to "mobiliz[e] [...] left-wing social conservatism against the disintegrating effects of the free market".[27] Doing so would ultimately hurt the advances made by the feminist movement, that is, in its essence, profoundly anti-nuclear family.

Unfortunately, this is already happening. Anti-sexual-liberation rhetoric is gaining momentum across the political spectrum. It manifests itself in reactionary manosphere content, in "common sense" feminism and in centrist/apolitical media.

Chapter 1
The Will to Not Change

The Manosphere

I would argue that the manosphere is part of the conservative ecosystem and embodies its most reactionary form. In fact, the manosphere has become a gateway through which newcomers can be drawn into conservative or even far-right politics. Its misogyny, racism, fatphobia, homophobia, transphobia and ableism are extremely raw. As previously mentioned, the manosphere gathers together pick-up artists, incels and men's rights activists, as well as the thinkers and gurus who influence them. It uses a specific language to classify men and women according to their mating potential. A man can be an incel (involuntary celibate), a normie (also called a cuck), or an alpha (a leader who naturally attracts women, also called femoids). As an example, a pick-up artist is often a normie that uses a set of strategies to attract women in order to be as successful as an alpha. On social media, pick-up artist videos like "The Art of Seduction Inspired by Human Psychology" or "Psychological Tricks That Turns Women On|Make Women Want You With Non-Compliance" gets hundreds of thousands of views from, I assume, average-looking to unattractive men struggling to find a girlfriend or someone to be intimate with.

Pick-up artists give the impression that women's psychology can be hacked, that dating is like a video game where you must select the right dialogue boxes to make the exchange successful and move on to the next step. "If a woman says this, then say that", "if a woman docs this, it means that". Now, learning how to analyse and respond to social cues (verbal and physical) is not problematic. Those of us who struggle with communication because of neurodivergence or simply because of bad communication skills can benefit a lot from this. However, it is problematic when an interlocutor feels entitled to a specific response and reacts negatively when they don't get it. Pick-up artist videos often show the pick-up artist performing the strategies they recommend in public spaces. Unsurprisingly, they only show when they succeed, and therefore viewers presume that using their strategy is always going to be successful. But human interactions are extremely complex and cannot be reduced to a set of secret hacks, and when the hacks don't work, rejection can build up into resentment.

The term "incel", short for involuntary celibate, was coined in 1997 by Alana, a bisexual woman, in order to describe her own sexual inactivity with others.[1] She did not anticipate, however, how the term would later evolve to represent one of the most reactionary communities on the internet. Incel communities are largely made up of white, Western men who are more or less connected to the alt-right ideology.[2] On incel forums, some users are seen reclaiming "what is rightfully theirs", meaning the right to engage in sexual activity with women, or to be in a relationship with a woman. Such rhetoric echoes sociologist Sylvie Laurent's definition of the "poor little white man"[3] that is related to the myth of racial dispossession.[4] The image of the "poor little white man" conveniently frames alt-right supporters as a group of people who have been left behind and silenced by the liberal left, which is too preoccupied with identity politics and prey to minority lobbying. It's a form of identity politics that alt-right commentators (like those at *The Daily Wire*) and politicians (like Trump, Farage, Bolsonaro, Le Pen or Meloni) use as part of their culture wars agenda.

Incels have forged a culture and language that has trickled down into mainstream internet culture and Gen Z vocabulary. "Stacys" are the tall, blond, sexually active, white women they can't access because of their unattractiveness. "Chads" are the strong-jawed, tall, handsome, white men that have unlimited sexual access. Those are obviously caricatures that are part of the irony of meme culture, and internet culture in general, but they serve to frame the incel as a persecuted minority. In an interview with Piers Morgan, Jordan B. Peterson started tearing up as Morgan described incels in harsh terms. Peterson defended them, saying "I thought the marginalised were supposed to have a voice".[5] One can feel empathy for lonely young men who "took the red pill" — a phrase inspired by the film trilogy *The Matrix*, in which main character Neo is given the option of taking the red pill, which would prepare him to be "unplugged" from the illusion of the Matrix. Taking the red pill therefore means choosing to open one's eyes to reality. In the case of incels-to-be, it is the realisation that they are not desirable according to Western desirability standards and that this will limit their chances of having sex. One can also feel empathy for those on the path of taking "the black pill", which is the realisation that their loneliness and undesirability cannot be overcome and that their existence will be miserable to the point of not being worth living. In *Men Who Hate Women*, Laura Bates shared a conversation she witnessed on an incel forum that made her feel empathetic towards those involved. The man described "the drudgery of his daily life, caring for a seriously disabled parent, unsupported by friends or wider family, frequently finding himself covered in urine and faeces". He went on to explain how he was abused as a child by his own parents to the point that it made him permanently disfigured. However, a few minutes later, Bates found herself in a different discussion in which the same user wrote: "I wouldn't feel like a real man if I had consensual sex. Rape is the alpha method of pleasure and procreation and foids [females] know this, that's why they prefer to get raped."[6]

Evaluating incels' victimhood demands that we consider *what* they are victims of, not *who* they are victims of. Within the incel community, liberated, picky women are said to be the problem. They are described as "hypergamous", a concept popularised by Jordan B. Peterson, which implies that they date and marry upwardly, leaving the least attractive and most precarious men celibate. They are therefore seen as responsible for the loneliness of the bottom tier men. Infamous incel mass shooter Elliot Rodger's hatred for women surpassed his hatred for the men who get access to women he cannot. "Men, after all, hate women so that they don't have to hate themselves", writes Katherine Angel.[7] In the video he published before the shooting, Rodger was openly racist and misogynistic. He exposed the politics of desirability in the most brutal way, forming a hierarchy of worthy and unworthy individuals based on appearance. The resentment he felt came from his conviction that he deserved a girlfriend, and some other men didn't, but he was alone, and they weren't.

In fact, incels tend to project the way they value women (physical attractiveness) onto themselves. They believe all women want is an attractive, chad-like guy because all they want is an attractive woman. In order to become more attractive, some incels go onto the Looksmaxxing Forum, which gathers "the most comprehensive and well-researched information on how you can improve your overall appearance".[8] Generally speaking, "looksmaxxing" refers to things like going to the gym or practising jaw exercises. If that is not enough, some men opt for "hardmaxxing", which involves plastic surgery. On the Looksmaxxing Forum, teenagers and young adults ask others to rate them in all honesty and describe their facial defects. This obsession with physical appearance is rooted in their undisputable belief in fixed biological realities, evolutionary theory and statistical reports on male attractiveness.

It would be dishonest not to admit that looks play an important role in dating, especially among teenagers and young adults. However, a partner's attractiveness is not the be all and end all of relationships. We have evolved from our ape era — we communicate, we can develop hobbies and interests that help us connect with each other and potentially want to date each other. Some incel communities include those aspects into their approach to self-improvement, but those communities are still marginal. Also, desirability extends far beyond evolutionary biology to the point of making it almost insignificant. What is deemed desirable is first and foremost established by what is socially valued. That is why the politics of desirability intersect with racism, ableism, fatphobia, etc.

The second source of victimhood within incel communities — that is a by-product of not appearing desirable — is the lack of sexual status. Amia Srinivasan believes that "incels aren't angry about their lack of sex, but about a perceived lack of sexual status".[9] Chads get to have sex with as many women as they wish, which gives them a certain status among men. Incels have been denied by women the possibility to even compete with chads, because of their looks.

While a significant number of incels do preach men's entitlement to sex and sexual violence, it is important to note that most of them go on the forums simply looking for tips on how to self-improve. That is why it is crucial to highlight the continuum between the manosphere and online self-help. Online self-help gurus define success by three pillars: financial freedom, health and fitness, and sexual status. I remember watching YouTube self-help guru Stefan James from *Project Life Mastery* and found it funny to see how often he would present his partner as one of his many achievements. "Here's my beautiful wife Tatiana", he would say, looking at the camera as if he was expecting some sort of applause or words of affirmation from his audience. "Here's my trophy wife Tatiana", would probably be a better transcription of what Stefan tried to convey. It relates in a way to what mega guru Anthony Robbins once wrote in *Awaken the Giant Within* to impress his readers:

> I discovered a magical power in me to take back control of my physical well-being. I permanently rid myself of 38 pounds of fat. Through this dramatic weight loss, I attracted the woman of my dreams. I married her and I created the family I'd always desired. I used my power to change my income from subsistence level to over ten million dollars a year. This moved me from a tiny apartment where I was washing my dishes in the bathtub, because there was no kitchen, to my family current home, the Spanish-style Del Mar castle.[10] *[Which is pictured in the book to satisfy the reader's curiosity.]*

In the era of self-actualisation, women are one of the many tools that allow heterosexual men to increase their social status. Marrying a good-looking, young, feminine and respectable woman is a sign of personal success. However, finding that ideal woman may not be as easy. Philosopher Alain de Botton once joked about the fact that self-help books like those from Anthony Robbins are often located in the same section as books on how to cope with depression, anxiety, loneliness, or self-hatred. The false promises of self-help gurus create deception that can lead to unhappiness, and, again, resentment.

So, incels are victims of two things: the politics of desirability and a resulting lack of sexual status. The first form of victimhood is legitimate, the second one could be (because men aren't born with a desire for sexual status, it is something they internalise as they grow up), but it cannot, because it reduces women to sexual objects, helping men build confidence and look good to other men. Some have also argued that incels suffer from a lack of intimate connection, which must be true for some of them, #notallincels. However, I would advise those who believe so to really look at what incels have to say about "femoids" on their forums. Once that is done, it is difficult to believe that any of them would want to interact with women for something different than the possibility of increasing their social status.

While incels tend to project superiority in the way they talk about and to women, their behaviour is revealing of deep insecurity. In a *Jubilee* video confronting a group of men's rights activists with a group of feminists, Derrick, a self-proclaimed incel, asserts that "women are a bit lost", and proceeds to compare them to children, to which a feminist replies that she doesn't need him, she can take care of herself.[11] This feeling of insecurity around independent women is not just an incel problem, however, it's a societal problem reflected in the media we consume. Jonathan McIntosh, known online as @ popculturedetective, analysed what he called the "born sexy yesterday" trope in sci-fi movies like *The Fifth Element* or *Tron: Legacy*.[12] In both cases, the protagonist is a rather lonely young man — a nice, handsome guy that doesn't fit in and struggles to communicate with others. The female protagonist, on the other hand, is either an AI or from another planet. In other words, she is not like the other girls. Korben Dallas (*The Fifth Element*) and Sam Flynn (*Tron: Legacy*) bond with Leeloo and Quorra respectively precisely because these women are different. In fact, these relationships are based on two things: 1) the lonely male character doesn't get the attention of modern women, doesn't particularly seek it, and doesn't have many male friends; and 2) the woman isn't yet corrupted by the modern world like most Western women are and she can act a bit childish which makes it easy to take control over her. These women are almost given to them. They aren't picky or demanding, they barely speak their language and can only trust *them*. In other words, this sci-fi trope sounds like an incel fantasy because the nice, lonely guy is rewarded with a cool, hot and fun girlfriend.

In defence of misunderstood, insecure men, philosopher and alternative self-help guru Alain de Botton further blamed women for disregarding what is now popularly called "the nice guy". In a fictional video titled "Why Nice People Are Scary" produced by de Botton's *The School of Life*, a female character says she struggles to find a nice partner.[13] She then meets a "nice guy" with whom she goes on a couple of dates before getting bored and going back to a toxic guy that clearly doesn't care about her. After thinking about it for a while, she eventually goes back to the "nice guy", who has been waiting for her this whole time. The argument that women do not want nice guys (a category of men Elliot Rodger and other incels claim to be a part of), and systematically go for the toxic ones, is once again reflected in the media we consume. The book and TV series *Twilight*, the movie *After*, and Lana Del Rey's songs are all examples of that. On social media, a plethora of young men capitalise on other men's insecurity and women's supposed pickiness. In a TikTok video that scored almost one million views, attractive content creator Zach Barbour told viewers why he "would make a bad boyfriend", while sitting in a trampoline.[14] Well, he's a nice guy, he says "I love you" way too much, he could talk to his girlfriend 24/7, etc. In the comments section, many other men related to what Zach said and shared his frustration. Ultimately, such content fosters the idea that women are the problem: they want a nice guy, but they reject them for toxic ones.

The world of self-help has tried to intellectualise the "nice guy" problem. In one of his lectures, Jordan B. Peterson explained that nice guys are characterised by agreeableness, which is considered a female characteristic.[15] He also recognised that most men and women can be both agreeable and conscientious, so his argument doesn't hold water.[16] Also, in a video published by the popular self-help YouTube channel *Charisma on Command*, with the words "DON'T BE NICE" written on its thumbnail, host Charlie analysed Joe Rogan's rhetoric and body language. He concluded that people should use Rogan as a role model because no woman wants a nice guy who people-pleases and is incapable of commanding respect. In other (incel) words, the nice guy is a cuck. He gives beta energy.

In conclusion, the entirety of the self-help industry (the

manosphere, hard-core self-help, alternative self-help) has failed to provide an answer to young men's loneliness that doesn't ultimately put the blame on women. Most gurus and influencers perform relatability only to capitalise on young men's insecurity in order to sell them books, courses and whatnot. Charlie from *Charisma on Command* even marketed himself as "a normal guy, voted shyest person in his graduating class in high school", on his website.[17] So, if he did it, you can do it too!

On the other hand, women have become quite sceptical of "nice guys". The YouTube channel *The Take* describes the "nice guy" trope on screen as that of a seemingly hopeless romantic who will go to extremes to get a girl's heart or have sex with her.[18] His niceness is motivated by the reward of a relationship or sexual favours — it is mostly fake. However, the existence of the negatively connoted "nice guy" stereotype does not mean women dislike guys who behave nicely, quite the contrary. In her show *Quarter Life Crisis*, comedian Taylor Tomlinson laughed that she finds it so sexy when a man respects the fact that she wants to wait before having sex that it makes her want to have sex with him. "There is nothing hotter than someone respecting your boundaries",[19] she concluded. (Also, who said women were picky? The bar is ten feet under the floor.) Conversely, in what turned out to be a parody of a documentary on a pick-up artist course, French comedian Bertrand Usclat and his team made fun of fake male feminists. Dressed as the pick-up artist, Usclat explained that "there exists one technique to seduce women, even better than money, a nice car, or a nice flat, and it's called feminism". He adds, "Yes, the course is expensive, but you'll very quickly compensate for that since you'll only meet women who refuse to let you pay the bill".[20]

Jokes aside, the aim of this section isn't to figure out if the blame should be put on men or women. As mentioned previously, we are the products of a patriarchal system that is making us very unhappy. The growing media sympathy given to lonely young men has led young women to also share their experience of loneliness, sexual deprivation and their inability to find a partner.[21] Breaking news! The politics of desirability also negatively impacts women and enbies (non-binary people). We are all victims of patriarchy in one way or another, but men also take advantage of it, and it is essential to continue to highlight that significant difference.

Toxic Masculinity (And Toxic Femininity?)

For social movements to grow and make an impact in society, it is necessary to transform emotions — feelings of anger, sadness, or injustice — into speech. Academia has always been closely related to activism precisely because it created the frameworks and concepts through which one could express feelings of injustice in an articulate manner. Toxic masculinity is one of them. It works according to the motto "the personal is political" because it politicises a set of behaviours and/ or speech acts performed by men into something that is constitutive of a larger societal problem. Thanks to this, people of all genders can better spot individual acts of violence or wrongdoing happening in their everyday lives and consider their systemic character. Toxic masculinity has helped a significant number of women understand patterns of violence in their own relationships and potentially leave before it was too late.

Many people across the political spectrum reject the concept of toxic masculinity because of its implication that every man is inherently toxic, or that masculinity is pathologized. As was argued in Part I, most feminists do not believe in essentialism, meaning they don't believe there is something *essentially* wrong about cis men and something *essentially* good about cis women. However, they believe in patterns that are mediated by a patriarchal culture and internalised by people across the gender spectrum, and toxic masculinity is one of them. The controversiality of toxic masculinity also reveals a certain degree of laziness. When people systematically understand accusations of toxic masculinity as attacks on the essence of men, they conveniently close the door to the possibility of change, because essence cannot be altered. For instance, Richard V. Reeves complains in *Of Boys and Men* that toxic masculinity "now refers to any male behaviour that the user disapproves of, from the tragic to the trivial".[22] The way Reeves argues his disapproval of the phrase toxic masculinity lacks perspective. He plays the game of reactionaries who solely rely on a few college campuses and classroom anecdotes to make their point. Those anecdotes are *systematically* told from the perspective of the accused, the respectable student, the innocent schoolboy who did something wrong but does not fully grasp why and therefore becomes the victim. The real victim, on the other hand, is never considered. Reeves probably forgot that women have accompanied men — partners, fathers, grandfathers, children — in becoming better, less aggressive, less commanding human beings for centuries now. Women, including feminists, have shown a path towards healthier forms of masculinity and continue to do so.

These anecdotes, which conveniently reverse the wrongdoer-victim paradigm, foster the idea that a feminised society seeks to pathologize masculinity. That is why some anti-feminists authentically believe that "men are trash" leads to "kill all men". However, I want to believe most men understand what feminists mean when they say "men are trash", or the other unnecessarily controversial slogan "I believe her". It is however more opportune to pretend they don't, to remain in denial because of anti-feminist sentiments, misogyny, or out of fear at the prospect of having to tackle the elephant in the room —patriarchy. Unfortunately, sceptics and anti-feminists take up a lot of mainstream media space, spreading the idea that feminists are anti-men extremists. Instead, that space could be used by women's rights advocates to better educate people on the distinction between an essentialist mode of thinking (men are inherently toxic, kill all men) and a social constructivist mode of thinking (men are socialised in a way that legitimises toxicity or sexual violence, so there is potential for change).

Once that distinction between essence and social construction is made clear, it is interesting to look at how the concept of toxic masculinity has been integrated into our culture. Because of the tendency to spot toxic masculinity in individual behaviours, it is expected from problematic individuals to work on themselves in order to overcome it. As a Black heterosexual man once commented under one of my videos, "learning how our position in society impacts others is the first step in learning true humility", with which I couldn't agree more. His comment was about the benefits of embracing feminism as a man (and the struggle he had with white American feminism, which has often lacked that very humility he mentioned). Unsurprisingly, the worlds of self-help and new age spirituality — which seek to distance themselves from politics to recentre on the self — have taken on the task of tackling the issue of toxic masculinity.

In fact, the phrase "toxic masculinity" was coined in the

1980s and 1990s by the mythopoetic men's movement, which sought to revive the "deep masculine" self.[23] The movement gained popularity after the release of Robert Bly's bestselling book *Iron John: A Book About Men*, which told the story of a boy maturing into adulthood with the help of a wild man. Writers and thinkers of the mythopoetic men's movement were influenced by Jungian psychology, which tends to regard gender as a biological reality attached to the psyche of men and women. The movement claimed that men no longer saw themselves as comrades celebrating their masculinity together. Instead, they became emotionless and greedy competitors. They believed men's voices were increasingly silenced by the rise of the feminist movement. Finally, they realised that men spent too much time with their wives which prevented them from developing that so-called deep masculinity.[24] One contemporary example of what they defined as toxic masculinity would be self-proclaimed alpha male influencer Andrew Tate. His misogyny is raw. He hates women so much that he doesn't even enjoy having sex with them anymore. He has also been accused of sex-trafficking and has admitted on camera that he took advantage of his numerous girlfriends for financial gain.[25] Andrew Tate blew up on social media in the matter of a few months and redirected that attention into his MLM-inspired Hustlers University. He ticks a lot of the toxic, immature man boxes defined by the mythopoetic men's movement: he didn't grow up with a masculine figure in the home as his father was mostly absent, he doesn't show any emotions except aggressiveness, he doesn't see other men as comrades but as competitors he must put down to lift himself up.

To counter toxic masculinity, the mythopoetic men's movement chose to organise homosocial retreats where men could reconnect with their true masculine self before going back to the egomaniacal liberal society that had corrupted them. To be clear though, the mythopoetic men did not invent the concept of restorative homosocial retreats. Twenty years before the movement was born, the infamous *Moynihan Report* on the Black family drew similar conclusions. Moynihan claimed that "the Negro community has been forced into a matriarchal structure [...] and imposes a crushing burden on the Negro men". He therefore advised that Black men get away from Black matriarchs and join the military, a homosocial environment where discipline, order and performance are glorified. The report was ridiculed by women's activists of the time, who wondered if encouraging men to join a systemically racist institution like the army was really going to boost Black men's deep masculinity.[26]

Going back to the mythopoetic men's movement, its advocates assured that once men have recovered their masculinity — that is coherent with the archetype of the good, family-oriented patriarch — they could then unleash their animal-male, command authority and maintain order.[27] In fact, deep masculinity seeks to reconnect with men's (supposed biological) nature, which includes violence. That is why the movement condemned feminism. Feminists sought to cancel this natural violent instinct instead of letting men learn how to control it by themselves, with the help of other men. In numerous lectures and interviews, Jordan B. Peterson discusses the inherent male struggle between violence and control in the same way the mythopoetic men's movement did. He identifies men's tendencies towards violence, which he relates to their higher level of testosterone, and frames it as something that is inherent to men's identity formation but also beneficial to society. According to him, "being able to be cruel and then not be cruel is better than not being able to".[28] Likewise, Trump advisor Stephen Bannon wrote that "these guys, these rootless white males, have monster power".[29] On social media, conservative commentators like Steven Crowder have warned feminists multiple times that, if things go too far, there will be more and more misogyny (in physically violent forms?)[30]

The mythopoetic men's movement isn't dead. A similar organisation, the ManKind Project, still exists today. On their official website, the ManKind Project is described as "a personal development organization that offers life-changing experiential training and support groups for all kinds of men".[31] During initiatory weekends, participants are asked to get rid of all their possessions, including their cell phone and car keys. They are completely isolated from the world, their names can be replaced by numbers, they eat very little, don't sleep much and are often asked to all get naked in public.[32] The experience ended up being traumatic for many participants and their close relatives. Several participants' partners shared to Miviludes (a French governmental organisation meant to keep an eye on the development of cults) that when their husband or boyfriend came back home after the retreat, their personality had changed for the worse. A woman said that her partner suddenly asked to divorce and became more aggressive with their kids.[33] At the ManKind Project, "toxic masculinity" is also connected to boyhood's immaturity. Deep masculinity cannot be achieved without a process of initiation by wiser, older, male figures. On social media, someone like Jordan B. Peterson has taken on the role of being a mentor to young, lost and "immature" men.

Now, I want to pause for a second because I suspect some of you do not understand what is wrong with wanting men to be more mature and responsible. Isn't that what constitutes healthy masculinity? To answer those concerns, let's take the example of Pablo Servigne, a French collapsologist whose work on the collapse of industrial societies has been translated in several languages. In *Another End of the World Is Possible*, he praised the ManKind Project and its female equivalent, Women Within, as tools to reconcile our masculine and feminine sides in the prospect of building a post-collapse society. This should ring a bell, since we have already talked about masculine and feminine essences in the section on divine femininity in Part I. In fact, the same criticism can be applied here. The belief in feminine versus masculine energies inevitably essentialises personality traits into two gendered categories in a way that strengthens already existing gender roles. That is why the ManKind Project, meant to forge "new warriors", is for men, and Women Within, whose name signals the feminine principles of receptiveness and self-care, is for women. It is true that we clearly need to rekindle the values of mutual aid and cooperation as part of our fight against climate change, but why do it in a gendered way? The ManKind Project and Women Within attract participants because, for the duration of a few days, individuals have no other objectives than to bond with other people, be creative and have fun. They are like adult summer camps, and we desperately need more of those.

I taught tennis for many years to kids and adults, and always assumed that adults expected me to only do technique-based lessons because they paid a good amount of money and were therefore expecting to see results. Once (out of laziness, let's be honest) I tried with them one of the games I typically did with kids, which consisted of a little story with points and teams and forfeits and secret rules. The truth is that they absolutely loved it, and regularly asked me to do it again. That weekly hour and a half at tennis was for them the chance to reconnect with the innocence and genuine camaraderie of their childhood and adolescent years. Each week, they stretched out those sessions for as long as they could, with a few after-lesson drinks at the bar. That was the experience of male/father players though. Women/mother players enjoyed those sessions just as much as men but were expected to go back home and take of care of their kids right after.

While there are a lot of positive things to draw from those observations I've made, the fact that it was conditioned by the payment of the tennis club's subscription and that men and women did not get the same experience because of gender inequality means that there is still a lot of work to do. We need to develop more public structures dedicated to leisure where camaraderie between people across the gender spectrum is nurtured and gendered expectations, like having to rush back home to cook dinner for the kids because honey doesn't know how to cook (as one of the female players once said), are obsolete.

Servigne's promotion of the ManKind Project and Women Within, on the other hand, is coherent with the belief that society should be run according to natural laws, meaning that in order to restore what has been broken, we have to reconcile with our natural selves. Following this logic, so-called experts seek to educate people on what those natural selves might look like by comparing human beings to various animal species. For instance, redpillers (some of the most reactionary members of the manosphere), including the infamous Rollo Tomassi, use apes as inspiration for how humans should run society. Now, the research on apes is conflicting because, like human beings, ape communities have different cultures. As an example, the belief that groups of chimps or baboons are ruled by an aggressive alpha male is not as consensual as redpillers want us to think. As soon as the field of research diversified in the late 1960s-1970s, women anthropologists, biologists and psychologists like Jane Goodall, Barbara Smuts, Shirley Strum, Vinciane Despret and others did not observe what they were taught to observe. For instance, they noticed that female baboons also had responsibilities that could sometimes put them above their male counterparts. Males, on the other hand, regularly sought the affection and friendliness of females to better integrate. Some scientists also observed that when two males fought for food, females tended to side with the male who lost the fight and rejected the one who won. Males were therefore encouraged not to compete for food but rather to share it.[34] Of course many argued that these women scientists were motivated by a feminist agenda, while men's research was assumed to be objective. Goodall, Smuts, Strum and Despret received diplomas and recognitions, just like their male colleagues, but "man" is the default, neutral, and "woman" equals gender bias.

Wolves are another species that have caught the attention of redpillers. The hierarchy of "alpha", "sigma" and "beta" wolves within a pack is used as the basis for the formation of hierarchies among men. However, the existence of such a hierarchy has also been debunked many times. Even Dave Mech, the scientist who helped popularise it, later campaigned to stop printing his work.[35] He and other scientists made a terrible mistake. They only observed wolves in captivity fighting for leadership in a limited territory.[36] They omitted that wolves adapt to their environment, like any other living being does. When observed in the wilderness, wolf packs consist of two parents and their puppies, whose co-dependency ensures their survival. Lone wolves are lonely until they fulfil the duty of finding a mate and a new territory. They better be quick at it because they can't survive by themselves for long. In other words, there is no such thing as the eternal "lone wolf", translated as the sigma male, also called the "Keanu Reeves" type.

So male aggressiveness, often linked to the production of testosterone, is not as natural as it seems. A recent scientific study published by the Proceedings of the National Academy of Sciences even concluded that testosterone could promote altruistic behaviours that enhance the male's social status.[37] In the end, believing that men need to reconnect with a form of deep masculinity that respects their natural tendency towards violence sounds to me like someone trying to find excuses not to do the work. Men don't need to be warriors, they simply need to be normal human beings, to do what they think is good according to them as human beings. There is no need to apply gendered expectations to that.

Now let me tell you about the animal species I studied for a very long time: kids. As I've just mentioned, I worked part-time as a tennis instructor for about seven years and spent countless hours watching hundreds of kids and adults from the age of three up to sixty interact with each other through sports. My observations aren't meant to establish *the truth*, but I thought it would be interesting to share my experience. One positive thing I noticed is that every year, boys would be less and less judgmental towards girls, but that doesn't mean they were not judgmental at all. Every time a mixed team lost, it had to be because of the girl, even if she had scored more points than, let's say, another boy. I had some discipline problems with boys who would shout at each other, throw their rackets away when they lost a game, hit other people with their rackets, including girls' bottoms, and refuse to play if they decided to. I thought for quite some time that I was the problem. I thought I wasn't commanding respect despite my occasional standing-tall (I'm 5'10), feet-shoulder-width apart, chest-up look coupled with my signature murderous stare. I certainly had a few more discipline problems than my older male colleagues, but they had a lot of problems too, and boys were always involved.

What struck me throughout the years is how entitled boys felt to disrupt their surrounding environment, while girls seemed to be way more conscious of their interactions with others and how they occupy space. Given what I have just explained, you could think I hated every single boy I ever trained, but it could not be further from the truth. Some boys were as respectful as girls, others were extra adorable with feminist ally potential, as I used to tell my colleagues. I treated each player equally, remained very open-minded and as calm as possible even when faced with the worst bullies. Finding positive tennis role models to compare to them to seemed to work quite well. Unfortunately, I only saw those kids an hour and a half per week, and that wasn't enough to compensate for what happened during the rest of it.

From the age of eighteen to twenty-one, I also played with a group mostly composed of adult men. The way toxic masculinity was performed was different yet still related to what I observed with the kids. When the number of women in the tennis club would decrease, the men would start speaking loudly, manspreading and commenting on women's physique. Often, I was the only woman in the room after tennis practise. The men got drinks, and I remained there, out of politeness, for ten to fifteen minutes. I felt extremely bad every time one of them would say something racist, homophobic or sexist.

It felt weirdly exaggerated, as if they were trying to get validation from others, as if those comments reinforced their masculinity.

Once, one joked about forcing his wife to have sex with him, what is called marital rape. Another time, a group of married men had fun asking me questions about the personal life of a female tennis player — who happened to be more than twenty years younger than them —which I refused to answer. A regular player also sexually harassed multiple (adult and teenage) women, collected women's numbers in the office of the tennis club and routinely waited for one of my female tennis colleagues to finish work, often alone, in the dark. The club only expelled him when he had an altercation with a tennis instructor over wanting to have sex with his wife in the middle of a lesson followed by a large group of parents. The financial loss (several parents removed their kids from the club after the incident) and the cost to the reputation of the club were finally good enough reasons to get rid of him.

When I went back there after the "incident", I was astonished to hear that some men wanted him to come back. One even joked that "we should find him an African woman" to satisfy his needs, I assume… Empathy, they called it, "he's struggling". I couldn't believe it, it was a complete lack of empathy for the women (me included) who, for years, did not feel safe when this man was around. Once again, I was caught up in an almost homosocial discussion where my arguments as to why this man is dangerous were half-heard or mocked. It was only when I told them I encouraged a friend to report him to the police that they became quiet and listened to me for a second. Now tell me and other women for whom this story sounds way too relatable that "toxic masculinity" does not exist. That those are individual cases of men acting on their so-called biological impulses rather than a system that allows them to disrespect women, and sometimes encourages them to do so, and protects them when they do.

The homophobic, racist, misogynistic or fatphobic homosocial discussions I witnessed and grew up with are now happening online. The political correctness that these men tend to adopt as they step out of those homosocial circles has completely disappeared. The language of the manosphere has become mainstream. Hate speech is raw now.

A concern of people who seek to establish a balance between misogynistic ideologies and the feminist response to them (if balance there ought to be) is that we ask men to change too quickly. Michelle Goldberg confessed in an article for the *New York Times* that she "feel[s] bad for a lot of the men caught out by the #MeToo movement". She said, "I can only imagine how disorienting it must be to have the rules change on you so fast",[38] to which Amia Srinivasan responded:

This idea — that the rules have suddenly changed on men, so that they now face punishment for behaviour that was once routinely permitted — has become a #MeToo commonplace. The implication seems to be that, until very recently, men had been subject to a totalising patriarchal ideology, one that made it impossible for many of them to tell the difference between flirtation and harassment, coquettishness and refusal, sex and rape.[39]

This is the convenient and complicit ignorance that is at the heart of a concept like toxic masculinity and that we hear in things like "boys will be boys", "he's always been a seducer", "he loves women", "he can be a bit problematic at times but he's a great guy/friend/colleague/father". On July 14, 2020, French President Emmanuel Macron was questioned by journalists on his decision to promote Gérald Darmanin, accused of rape and sexual abuse of a victim in a state of weakness, which he partly recognised, to Minister of the Interior. This was the same president that had declared during his 2017 campaign that the fight against gender inequality — including sexual violence — would be the "great cause" of his presidency. During the interview, he justified the promotion of Darmanin, saying that he had a conversation with him "man to man".[40] What does "man to man" mean? A couple of years later, he said the exact same thing for minister Nicolas Hulot, accused of rape and sexual assault.[41] Imagine how surprised I was when I went to the London Tate Library, scanned through a book of *The Big Idea* primer collection on toxic masculinity and read that "these leaders' [Obama, Trudeau and Macron] behaviour suggests they might identify as pro-feminist".[42] Macron's great cause was so great that he had to reconduct it for his second mandate with his bestie Darmanin.

The presumption of ignorance and the systematic individualisation of cases related to toxic masculinity have been challenged by the #MeToo movement. In fact, #MeToo was not just about the men who had abused women, children and other men. It also served to expose the networks of people who allowed for such things to be perpetrated. For every man accused, the entire structure in which he operated was questioned. For the first time, sceptics who automatically individualised cases were forced to see the systemic character of sexual violence. As French journalist Lauren Bastide explained, we were forced to understand that all parts of society are affected by it, that it happens everywhere, "at the doctor's office, in activist organisations, in political parties, in cleaning companies, in sports clubs, in the countryside, in cities, in affluent areas, in deprived areas, among left-wing people, among right-wing people…"[43]

But some continue to resist generalisations. In an interview with Jordan B. Peterson, which was viewed more than three million times on YouTube (mostly by his fans, judging by the content of the comments section), journalist Anne McElvoy sought to challenge him in the context of #MeToo. She succeeded in making him admit that beyond the person of Harvey Weinstein, there is a culture of sexual harassment and abuse in Hollywood. However, when she tried to make him expand that "cultural problem" beyond Hollywood, Peterson realised where she was going and the conversation on that topic stopped.[44]

When I searched for the interview on YouTube, entering the words "Peterson+McElvoy+interview", the second video I saw in the list of results was titled "Jordan Peterson Female BULLYING tactics & acted out by interviewer Anne McElvoy". In the thumbnail of the video there was a list including the following words:

- Verbal attack
- Innuendo
- Gossip
- Reputation destruction

These terms are often used to discredit the concept of toxic masculinity, as they imply that for every toxic masculine trait, there is a toxic feminine trait. Those traits are often assigned to women who have talked publicly about sexual assault or harassment, especially during the #MeToo trials, and most prominently during Amber Heard's trial, which triggered a wave of cyber-bullying powered by the manosphere. I refuse to believe in the existence of a form of toxic femininity that could be put on the same level as toxic masculinity and I'm going to explain why.

First, toxic femininity is defined — by those who use it — according to primitive instincts. Specifically, it is believed that in order to diminish someone else's reputation, men fight and women gossip. However, there is a crucial difference between the two. When a man wins a fight, he simultaneously diminishes the other man's status and increases his. He has proved his masculinity, he is strong, he can protect any woman, yada yada yada. When a woman gossips, she only diminishes the status of other women. She didn't prove any quality, it does not improve her social status but only hurts that of other women.

The second reason why I dislike this notion of toxic femininity is that it gives the impression that women hate each other more than they really do. Look at the common assumption that women hate their female boss. The assumption was popularised with the rise of the (hard to like) girlboss. When you google "women hate female bosses", you can find dozens of articles, posts and videos reasserting this very idea. Interestingly, most of those articles were published in the years following the release of the book *#Girlboss* by Sophia Amoruso (2014-2015) that also marked the beginning of the anti-girlboss backlash. However, when we look at the data, we understand that, no, women do not hate female bosses, quite the contrary. Gallup recorded Americans' preferences regarding the gender of their boss since the 1950s. Since 2017, most Americans do not have a preference and since

2014, women who say they have a preference have leaned towards a female boss.[45]

When I was teaching tennis, I also realised that girls would systematically stick together. Of course, group preferences are a natural thing, but even on test days, girls (including some who struggled to play well) would continue to stick together. On top of that, I noticed that girl players performed better at exercises that involved cooperation with other girls. It seemed like cooperation (not competition) with another girl encouraged them to do better. One could argue that this early-age sorority was motivated by the fact that our groups were overrepresented by boys. But when we look at the structure of our Western societies, men are also overrepresented in many spheres, especially in leadership and managerial positions. So, why aren't women showing more solidarity like the girls in my tennis groups? In fact, as they grow up, women understand that in order to gain power in a patriarchal society, they have to compete against each other for the attention of men.

On social media, people talk about the "pick-me" girl, the "not like the other girls" girl (nlogs). It refers to women who seek to differentiate themselves from a constructed group of "other women", often described as overtly feminine, gossipy, into make-up and clothes, not into sports or video games. The pick-me girl is the materialisation of internalised misogyny, which is defined as the tendency to diminish the value of other women and foster negative gender stereotypes. Other examples of internalised misogyny are to be found in the need to constantly compare female popstars like Rihanna and Beyoncé, Miley Cyrus and Selena Gomez, in slut-shaming, in the rivalry between mothers, in the way some women recklessly harassed Amber Heard, and, funnily enough, in the way women throw "pick-me" accusations at any woman.[46]

Internalised misogyny is detrimental to women. It prevents them from being promoted, from being taken seriously, it diminishes their self-confidence, it makes them lose friendships. The topic of women who hate women is a controversial one because, in an ideal feminist world, women would all support each other, but in reality, they don't.

To fight against internalised misogyny, women have been encouraged to connect with other women and forge sorority. As a recovering nlog, I have learned how to find beauty and strength in the women around me by sharing with them my struggles, fears and accomplishments. #MeToo also managed to build an entire movement around this concept of sorority, as its name indicates. But there is still a long way to go, and in all honesty, I don't think we should continue to romanticise sorority to the degree we do now. Sorority cannot completely erase the problem of women who hate other women, for two reasons. First, believing that women act in misogynist ways because they have internalised the norms of patriarchy tends to cancel women's agency. For example, every time conservative commentator Candace Owens says something misogynistic, she gets immediately accused of being the puppet of conservative men. Similarly, Brett Cooper is often called a conservative pick-me because of her controversial takes on feminism. Systematically, the agency of these women is taken away from them because of the assumption that women cannot be misogynistic. If they act like they do, that means they must be operating under the control of conservative men or patriarchy. However, both Owens and Cooper know exactly what they are doing. These women do not have the capacity for sorority because their conservatism precedes their identity as women.

The second reason why sorority will not solve the problem of women who hate women is that some women's definition of sorority is exclusionary — meaning that it shuts the door to women of a specific skin colour, a specific social background, a specific professional background or a specific gender identity. The existence of a phrase like "white feminism" puts into words the exclusionary feminism of certain white feminists. TERFs (trans-exclusionary radical feminists) exclude trans women. SWERFs (sex worker-exclusionary radical feminist) exclude sex workers.

In the end, sorority is a consciousness-raising tool that is essential to one's understanding of internalised misogyny and that should be promoted. However, its potential is limited by the fact that some women consciously reject it for personal and political gains, and others only practise it with specific groups of people.

To conclude, the concept of toxic femininity is flawed. Sorority — or at least neutrality — in women's relationships with one another is more common than we think, but is not sufficient to fully dismantle internalised misogyny. While it is true that patterns of toxicity between women can cause psychological damage, it must be stated that toxic femininity is not physically violent, or, to put it more bluntly, toxic femininity does not kill. We cannot compare gossip and verbal attacks to physical attacks like rapes, femicide, and other forms of violence imposed by men on (primarily) women. In fact, the rejection of toxic masculinity on the basis that toxic femininity exists is as valid as the invention of a female version of incels: "femcels". These are two completely different things. Femcels have never gathered 100,000 subscribers on a subreddit discussing eugenics, racism, rape and mass killings,[47] and have never done mass shootings like incels have. Most of them hate themselves more than they hate men.

While women seek to resolve the problems related to internalised misogyny through sorority, men who have the will to change have taken on the task to help other men develop healthier forms of masculinity. An increasing number of male celebrities, influencers and fictional male characters reject the dogmas of heterosexual macho masculinity, and it must be said that women and queer people love to see that. Funnily enough, on *Urban Dictionary* (on which any user can provide a definition that is then approved or disapproved by other users), the most popular definition for Timothée Chalamet reads as follows:

The reason I find the will to live every. single. day.

Rachel: Why can't they all be like Timothée Chalamet??
Monica: I KNOW RIGHT?!!

We know that role models are crucial in forming identity, including gender identity. If we ensure that men can identify to *Ideal-Is*, as Lacan called them, that promote healthy values, we can hope for drastic changes in the way men approach masculinity. However, as is the case with sorority, the glorification of men's conversion from toxic to healthy masculinity has its limits. First, healthy masculinity is still primarily understood through aesthetics. Putting on a skirt and a cardigan immediately turns you into a healthy masculinity guru. Now, don't get me wrong, gender expression is primarily perceived by others through the way one looks, and conversely one's looks are usually the visual representation of one's beliefs (think about what was said in Part I regarding aesthetics as forms of speech), but if we solely understand healthy masculinity through aesthetics, like liberal media tends to do, we barely scratch the surface of the problem. To put it simply, Timothée Chalamet looks like a softboy but could be a fuckboy. I sincerely hope he isn't, and I really do not want to be cancelled by his hardcore fans, but it remains a possibility. Jokes aside, it is crucial that we re-evaluate the criteria with which we define healthy masculinity.

Second, the goal shouldn't be to switch from one type of masculinity (toxic) to another type of masculinity (healthy/ positive), but rather to reject the idea that the formation of one's identity, meaning one's value system and tastes, can only be mediated through a fixed gender expression. In other words, it is reductive to attach a set of moral values (toxic or positive) to masculinity. Why do we tell boys to become good *men* and not just a good *people*? What does being good have to do with gender expression? To some degree, healthy masculinity becomes yet another box, one that signals modernity, that is deemed increasingly respectable and that grants symbolic rewards. It is time to imagine the formation of a man's identity outside the constraints of masculinity, outside the constraints of a fixed definition.

Our current obsession with finding healthy masculine role models for young men is not revolutionary but only reformist. There have always been male celebrity role models that have challenged traditional masculinity (David Bowie, Kurt Cobain, Prince, even 2Pac to some extent) but they did not, by virtue of existing, dismantle patriarchy. In one of his YouTube videos, Henry, known as LittleJoel, commented on a viral tweet that read as follows: "the reason why young men flock to alt right movements is because the left gives brain-dead advice to young men. We need to be more compassionate to them, for our own sake." Yes we do, replied Henry, but it is also naïve to believe that the problem is that the right words are not being said to them, that the right images aren't shown to them, and that if we simply edited all of that and came out with the right words and the right guy who says all the right things, then everything would be OK.[48] No, it is not as simple as that. Believing that is symptomatic of a tendency to reduce big structural problems to changes in individual behaviours. Sure, having more *hommes déconstruits* (as we say in French, which could be translated as "deconstructed men") is a good thing, but it is not enough.

Heterosexual Realism

In 1972, the Gay Revolution Party issued a statement in which they expressed concern for straight women who "seem to believe that through their attempts to create 'new men' they will liberate themselves".[49] Since the inception of the feminist movement, lesbians have kept heterosexual women (especially those who call themselves feminists) in check, and that is a good thing. It is always interesting to hear what individuals who don't like men have to say. Despite the many awful, degrading experiences I've had with men, the violence I experienced, despite going into a relationship thinking "OK, I can change him" and realising, often too late, that they were not going to change, I want to remain hopeful. Maybe because I have also had many positive experiences with men, friends or boyfriends, who had, as feminist bell hooks titled one of her books, *the will to change*.

While hooks sought to bridge self-knowledge with feminist

theory, it is primarily through the industry of self-help that people — mostly women — try to find solutions to fix their heterosexual relationships. In the US, Justin Baldoni has become *the* healthy masculinity guru, with 3.2 million followers on Instagram (see, healthy masculinity can be a profitable business too). His book *Boys Will Be Humans* hoped to popularise a movement that he, Liz Plank (known as @FeministFabulous on Instagram) and James Heath started with their podcast *Man Enough*. Love, compassion and understanding are central to the work he does. Justin is naturally friends with Esther Perel, the psychotherapist superstar whose TED Talks on love, infidelity and relationships have gathered millions of views. Her work was certainly a source of inspiration for *The School of Life*, an institution on YouTube that always gets a generous number of views on their "relationship" videos, most of them targeting straight people.

As you can see, there are countless books, talks, podcasts, videos and courses on how to improve heterosexual relationships. Heterosexual couples are willing to pay a lot of money to make their marriage last as long as in the Disney movies. Because of that, people who aren't straight are starting to wonder what is wrong with heteros. In 2019, the subreddit "Are the Straights OK?" was created. It has now more than 400,000 members and has served as a source of content for online commentators and entertainers. On it, you'll find videos of out of proportion gender reveals, memes of "marriage is hell" jokes, TikTok videos of "super straight" people or photos of straight prides. Making fun of straight culture is not a queer-people-only activity. Many heterosexuals love to indulge in the cringiness of hetero culture as a form of catharsis.

In a video essay on the topic,[50] Tara Mooknee highlighted an article written by Asa Seresin in which she defines "heteropessimism" as the "performative disaffiliations with heterosexuality, usually expressed in the form of regret, embarrassment, or hopelessness about straight experience".[51] This heteropessimism has now been replaced by a "heterofatalism", as people who have experienced the former rarely abandon heterosexuality. "Marriage is hell" jokes are symptomatic of heterofatalism, just like incels who love to mock straight culture and caricature straight people but simultaneously can't imagine living outside of it.[52]

"It's easier to imagine the end of the world than the end of capitalism", was used by Mark Fisher to capture the essence of what he called "capitalist realism". In a way, we could replace the word "capitalism" here with "heterosexuality". But in order to do so, we must understand heterosexuality, not as a fixed sexual preference, but rather as an entire system of norms and expectations. Queer theorists have called it "heteronormativity", Kate Millet talked about the heterosexual political system, Cherríe Moraga chose instead the institution of heterosexuality.[53] All these concepts point to the same thing, namely the imposition of heterosexual norms, including the nuclear family, onto individuals of all genders.

In *Family Values*, sociologist Melinda Cooper showed that, in the US, neoliberals and neoconservatives have worked together to reinforce the nuclear family through legislation. In order to reduce the welfare state, they had to transfer social support from the public to the private sphere. Thatcher's famous quote, "There's no such thing as society. There are individual men and women and there are families", and Reagan's "save our children" anti-gay propaganda served to preserve the self-sufficient caring unit that is the nuclear heterosexual family. As an example, the neoliberal myth of meritocracy cannot survive without the family. In fact, a large proportion of so-called "self-made" individuals come from already privileged families.[54] Those families, like the Kardashian/Jenner family, perpetuate the meritocratic myth by marketing themselves as "self-made" men and women and then proceed to enhance their family wealth, generation after generation. Real "self-made" people, who sociologist Chantal Jaquet calls "transclass", are extremely rare. Without these upper-middle-class and upper-class families, there probably would not be enough "self-made" stories to feed the myth.

Cooper's observations also manifest themselves in the type of media produced by neoliberal institutions. On Netflix, the successful show *Too Hot to Handle* is an example of how the imagery of sexual liberation simultaneously gets exploited and regulated in order to align with capitalist objectives. In the show, ten very hot and very sexually active male and female participants are sent to an exotic place where they interact with each other for about a month. The goal of the show is to help them form connections with other participants and build long-lasting relationships. The group starts with a $100,000 prize that gets reduced every time a participant breaks a rule. Kissing, sexual contact and self-gratification are all forbidden. Those who systematically break the rules or do not seem to form connections get kicked out by "Lana" — the cone-shaped virtual assistant located at different places in the house that acts like a dystopic, panopticon version of Alexa. On the other hand, those who behave well and form relationships are rewarded with special gifts, including the ability to kiss each other for a few seconds. If we remove the overtly sexual appeal of the show (participants appear with very little clothes on), the structure of it is rather conservative. Participants' sexual abstinence is rewarded with money and people's validation. In

Too Hot to Handle, the aesthetics of sexual liberation facilitate the introduction of conservative rules.[55]

Dating apps are also representative of this ambiguity. They are perceived by many as consumerist tools (neoliberalism) that foster hook-up culture (sexual liberation/disintegration of social structures, as Illouz would say), but let us not forget that they are also effective at forming monogamous heterosexual relationships. In other words, the neoliberal inventions that are dating apps create traditional social structures. In a study I conducted where I asked participants to share their positive experience with dating apps (serious and non-serious), 58% of them told me they had found a partner (61% of those 58% being heterosexual).[56] In addition to that, the aesthetic and marketing of these apps rely on the ideal of the soulmate. A match on Tinder is manifested by the visual assemblage of the two profiles connected into one. Dating apps ad campaigns almost always present a young monogamous (often heterosexual) couple living their best life together. Hinge even titled one of their campaigns, "The dating app designed to be deleted". Finally, other dating apps like Bumble or OkCupid allow users to be very specific in terms of what they are looking for in a partner to improve the chances of finding "the one".

Even consumerist events like Valentine's Day, Mother's Day, and Father's Day, serve to strengthen social structures through surveillance. Such capitalism-friendly events reinforce heteronormativity and the nuclear family. They act as reminders that, "Hey you're supposed to love your girlfriend/wife/mother/father today and celebrate your relationship!" The middle class loves to celebrate these events with dinners, parties and trips, and post them on social media. By doing so they (yes, share love, but also) seek validation for conforming to the norms of the heterosexual institution and indirectly put pressure on those who don't.

Now, queer couples also celebrate these events, so why do we call it a heterosexual institution? As mentioned at the beginning of this section, the "heterosexual" in heterosexual institution must be understood not as a sexual orientation but as a normative structure that favours the nuclear family. As Western societies became more inclusive, marginalised communities (people of colour, indigenous communities, LGBTQ+ communities) have been allowed, encouraged or forced to comply with the nuclear family model. The middle-class dream of the suburban house with its private garden became an inclusive capitalist fantasy.

In fact, improving one's financial status is one of the reasons why people get or stick together. In a conversation on the housing crisis between author Sophie Lewis and journalist and activist Ben Smoke, the latter commented that "specific market conditions really impact the speed of our relationships", that "£1,000 for a room [in London], on the wages that most people in the city are earning, is simply… you can't do it".[57] For the working class, city life is hardly accessible, and sometimes the suburban life in a flat or house is all they can afford, and it happens to be a mode of living that fosters isolation onto the family unit. On top of that, inflation has imposed new cuts on the budgets of working class people. On French TV, a representative of an anti-poverty organisation warned that some households could not afford to use their cars anymore and were therefore stuck at home. Another participant, a mayor, added that decreasing purchasing power prevented families from investing in leisure, and further isolated them into the private sphere.[58] Journalist Victoire Tuaillon also wondered whether partners are able to question themselves and their relationships when they are overworked.[59] In fact, the structure of the typical 9-to-5, five days a week work schedule limits social interactions outside the workplace and the home. If that was not clear enough, neoliberal policies strengthen the nuclear family by isolating people in the private sphere and displacing the duty of care onto the smallest unit possible.

In France, a study by the *Institut français d'opinion publique* (French Institute of Public Opinion) compared the division of house chores in the 1980s and 2011. Women went from taking care of 69% of house chores to 64%. Working-class women are more likely to take charge of the house chores.[60] The unequal division of labour as well as women's likeliness to stay at home, work part-time or slow down their career for family life is hardly compensated for. Because of this, women must think twice before leaving their partner or divorcing. Some women remain in unfulfilling or abusive relationships because they cannot afford to exit them or cannot imagine going back to work after a long pause. My parents separated over "emotional" reasons when I was eight. However, my mother didn't want to get a divorce because of the amount of money, work and energy it would have taken to enact all the work she did for the household (going part-time for three years and increasing the value of the house with her own hands). She instead calculated by herself how much all those investments would amount to and asked my father to progressively pay for it in the form of school tuitions and mortgage payments.

Fixing the problem on an individual level is the only option left to a lot of women who seek to detach themselves from heterosexual relationships. Some have even gone as far as completely giving up on heterosexuality. In Part I, I explained how the cottagecore aesthetic was appropriated by traditional living advocates. What I didn't mention is that queer communities have also, to a lesser degree, appropriated the trend. In an article in the *New York Times*, Isabel Slone said that "cottagecore offers a vision of the world where men are not consciously excluded; they are simply an afterthought".[61] Rachel, aka @faythegay, and other queer creators argue that cottagecore is "an opportunity for queer people to re-appropriate and "own" the traditional way of life that has often been denied from them".[62] Hitomi Mochizuki, a lifestyle vlogger with more than one million subscribers on YouTube, has made sacred sisterhood her brand. In multiple vlogs, she shares moments she spends surrounded by women in nature. She describes sacred sisterhood as a "deep intimacy with her sisters [...] a dynamic that no romantic relationship will ever replace".[63] The feeling of safety around other women, the sharing of the unspoken and the atmosphere of healing and growth are what drew her to make sacred sisterhood a pillar in her life. She compares her friendships with other women to romantic relationships (minus the sexual intimacy) in the sense that they show up for one another like a loving partner would. On Instagram, the sisters Julia and Anastasia Vanderbyl share their life in perfect harmony with nature, taking care of animals, cooking, gardening, creating, building and learning to live from the land without men. With more than 550,000 followers, the sisters' regenerative and slow lifestyle is a source of inspiration for many.

These experiences are related to one another through the value they give to *care*. According to philosopher Fabienne Brugère, the ethic of care starts with the recognition that no human being can be self-sufficient.[64] The notion of care is socially connected to womanhood but shouldn't be understood as its essence. Indeed, projecting care as an extension of the maternal bond is restrictive since it can only exist in a heterosexual context. On the contrary, care is a political project that has no gender.[65] But if we are to herald it as the core value of the society we want to create, we must be more specific with what we mean by *care*. In fact, we must be careful about the co-option of this now trendy notion by neoliberals. As an example, French President Emmanuel Macron claimed that he has "one rule of life, for women and for men as well as for structures: care".[66] However, the millions of French people who protested him and his government during his two mandates, including health workers, would certainly disagree. According to philosopher Angélique Del Rey, the way we understand care cannot extend beyond individualism towards a preoccupation with the common good.[67] In other words, a true ethic of care cannot exist under capitalism because it systematically privatises it.

Let's go back to the examples we used earlier to understand what care under capitalism looks like. Romanticised on social media, the ideal of the caring unit of sisterhood is either restricted to certain privileged groups or financially constrained. On the one hand you have seven upper-class girl friends build their dream retirement house in the green hills of suburban Guangzhou, China.[68] On the other hand, you also have a growing number of middle-aged (widowed, divorced or celibate) women who choose to live together like a modern-day version of the fourteenth-century *"beguines"* to save on food, energy and rent.[69] In the late nineteenth and early twentieth centuries, women also chose to live together and were said to enter a "Boston marriage" motivated by romantic friendships or closeted homosexuality.[70] The loosely defined structure of the Boston marriage allowed upper-class lesbians to live in accordance with their sexuality in the private sphere. Whether they do it by choice, by necessity or a combination of the two, women take care of each other in resistance to patriarchal capitalism.

In an article on "heterosexuality and its discontents", researcher Yuhe Faye Wang argues that "placing the responsibility for heterosexuality onto women reflects a wider trend that deflects responsibility for structural problems onto individual choices".[71] Women are expected to educate the men around them, support them while they change (Justin Baldoni himself recognised that his wife could have given up on him a lot of times, that he had made a lot of mistakes[72]) or to leave heterosexuality all together if they are not happy with it. In fact, it is common for oppressive systems to circumvent criticism by appropriating it in a way that makes them compatible with it.[73] In the article, Yuhe Faye Wang compares the personal responsibility of giving up heterosexuality to the personal responsibility of adopting sustainable habits like recycling. Likewise, Victoire Tuaillon has noticed how patriarchy has incorporated sexual liberation for its own benefits. She sees it in the way heterosexual men replicate sexist patterns in their practice of non-conventional relationships — including polyamory, situationships, etc. She is upset that some men use what she discussed in her podcast on modern love without properly questioning their sexist biases and therefore reproducing them in non-traditional relationships.[74]

If the neoliberal heterosexual institution traps us into the nuclear unit, privatises care and absorbs criticism to remain powerful, what we need then, is a revolution. Tuaillon, like bell hooks and many others before her, wants to launch a(n) (intersectional) love revolution.[75] In fact, love, as well as anger, shows one's ability to be affected by external causes. Spinoza wrote that the deeper the affection, the greater the power to act. Rhetorically speaking, adding the adjective "love" to "revolution" is convenient as it keeps its advocates mainstream-media-friendly. If they removed the term "love", those feminists would probably enter "crazy women" territory — meaning they would lose respectability. However, it is crucial not to repress negative emotions in social justice advocacy, for that negativity doesn't stem from envy (to be like the powerful) but justice (to abolish the structures that make some more powerful than others). Tuaillon compares the love revolution she wants to materialise to the romantic French Revolution of the late eighteenth century, probably with Delacroix's *Liberty Leading the People* in the back of her mind.[76] Plato used the term "*agápē*" to refer to this form of communal love. The potential of *agápē* is to be found in things like a passionate conversation with a friend: the type of conversation that makes you both feel extra powerful and can motivate you to start (a joint podcast or) a revolution.[77]

I spent two years researching urban Black communities in the US in the 1960s, especially the Black Panther Party (BPP) — a movement that was built on communal love, *agápē* — and I was intrigued by the encouragements activists would give to a speaker as they talked: "that's right", "amen", "get 'em", etc. You could see how those words of affirmation progressively galvanised the speaker and led them to places they probably wouldn't have gone without them. One could see anger on the faces of Huey Newton, Angela Davis and other Panther leaders, but that anger was powered by a love for justice.

Pussy Power

In 1969, the tensions between the two factions of the US activist organisation Students for a Democratic Society (SDS) grew. The Black Panthers were instrumentalised during the SDS National Convention to diminish the Progressive Labor (PL) faction that claimed to be the vanguard of the revolution and had made women's liberation a central element of its ideology. To defy them, BPP's Chicago Minister of Information Rufus "Chaka" Walls was invited to speak on the first night of the convention. He first hammered that the Black Panther Party was the true vanguard of the revolution, not the PL, and then inexplicably added that the Panthers supported free love and "pussy power". The PL crowd reacted very negatively to Walls' statement and started chanting "fight male chauvinism!"[78] As former Panther Elaine Brown recounted in her memoir, many male Panthers, like US society in general, were misogynistic.[79] Therefore, declaring that it supported "pussy power" to a crowd of progressive people, including feminists, felt offensive. It revealed left-wing men's blatant misunderstanding of what women's liberation means and made the SDS look ridiculous.

On *Urban Dictionary*, the most popular definition of the power of the pussy reads as follows:

The Power of the Pussy... This is the power that beautiful women have! When you are under control of her power you are in a trance like state and the only source of comfort is her Pussy. This power is activated after you have become one with her, and actually care very much about her. It's not just any pussy it HAS to be her, her persona...and everything else about her... The more you are attracted to the chick the stronger the pull to the warm piece of

Heaven between her legs. This force is inescapable, and can lead men to go totally Bizerrco! He might be tempted to buy her a ring, and forsake all other chicks, then the power has manifested itself. Rulers down through the ages have lost kingdoms because of this power and it has caused many forms of violence across the planet...

The user also provides a useful example:

Guy 1.. I can't stop thinking about her, she is using the power of the pussy on me I think I'm going ask her to marry me!

Guy 2.. Dude whats wrong with you? Go to the desert and take a handfull of mushrooms or something !

This sounds like a perfectly reasonable conversation, doesn't it? The pussy is sacralised into something that rules above morality and makes heterosexual and bi men lose their mind. In a series of street interviews conducted by the *It's Complicated* YouTube channel, a male interviewer asked several people, mostly partygoers, about the power of the pussy. Starting with a basic question, "Do you know what pussy power is?", to which most participants laughed, the interview quickly progressed onto more serious questions. The gap between the interviewer's seriousness and the interviewees' casualness helped the former get what he wanted from the interview. In fact, right after he got interviewees to approve pussy power was real — "I mean... OnlyFans", said one of the male participants; "I have all the privilege" joked a woman; "the world revolves around pussy, we run the world", said another — he proceeded to ask them why they think there is so much talk in our society about things like male privilege and white privilege, but never about pussy privilege? Interviewees couldn't argue against it without taking the risk of contradicting themselves. The interviewer therefore came to the conclusion he hoped for, namely that pussy power "is one of the most powerful privileges that exists [...] and it's never talked about [...] because it destroys the victim narrative".[80] The video has (as I'm writing) half a million views and thirteen thousand likes, and the comments are full of people sharing anecdotes of women who "took advantage of them" with their pussy power, obviously.

Refuting the existence of women's oppression because straight men lose control when faced with "pussy power" is far-fetched, but coherent with the manosphere's discourse which reduces women to sexual objects with rights. It is crucial to understand that, from a misogynist perspective, women's rights collide with men's entitlement to sex. Sexual status is only accessible through women, who can dictate who can have it and who cannot. It is precisely the power of consent and the possibility of rejection that frustrate the most radical incels. One can feel that frustration in the questions asked by the interviewer, who does not seem to like women very much. In fact, his obsession with pussy power made him look ridiculous to more than one participant who burst out laughing and responded ironically. Only two male participants went along with him to the point of asserting that "most of our economy has to do with women because of... pussy power" (big brain energy). Men buy things to please women, women buy things to get the attention of men, consumerism runs on pussy power. Interestingly, one of those two men concluded by saying that "this went from a regular interview to 'I'm starting to hate women'", which is exactly the aim of such content. It fosters misogyny.

Street interviews of this sort have become increasingly popular on social media. Anonymous straight men go to nightclubs and bars to interact with young women dressed for a night out and portray them as "low value" — to use the words of the *Fresh and Fit* podcast hosts. They want to assert the narrative that dumb Stacys, and by extension all women, are undeserving of the power they have to decide whether a man deserves their attention or access to their body. Remember that incel Derrick who compared women to children…

The idea presented in the *Urban Dictionary* definition that pussy power has caused a lot of violence across the globe is misconstrued. We must separate mythologies from actual history, and facts are clear about that — no powerful pussy has ever caused a war or revolution. Conflicts involving women were accompanied by economic, expansionist or community survival preoccupations, or were instrumentalised as part of ego clashes between men. In fact, women's sexuality has always been, across the globe, regulated by patriarchal control. Sure, liberal societies have progressively allowed women to reclaim power over their bodies and use sexual appeal for economic independence or empowerment, but that's very new, and never fully granted. "Pussy privilege" doesn't make any sense when put in perspective with the reality that is patriarchy. It remains a buzz phrase used to forge logical fallacies that ultimately serves to push a conservative agenda.

Why, then, do women talk about pussy power positively? In fact, "pussy power" has entered women's liberation vocabulary, from female rappers' lyrics to anti-Trump protests. The latter could be explained by the fact that former President Trump was once caught saying that when you're a star (like him, presumably) "you can do anything […] Grab them by the pussy." Using that phrase as a rallying cry against him sounded like an effective way for women to reclaim power over their bodies. Also, the rather recent demystification of the anatomy of people who menstruate has normalised the use of terms like "pussy", "vagina", "clitoris" within progressive spheres. Now that the stigma around those organs has been removed, they have been turned into art, designs that further normalise their existence. However, it must be noted that reducing a woman to her genitals tends to be essentialising and neglects the existence of trans women. It is not surprising that French TERFs (trans-exclusionary radical feminists) Dora Moutot and Marguerite Stern have called their movement "*Femelliste*", drawn from the word "*femelle*", female (only used in French to characterise animals) in order to exclude women who don't have the right reproductive system, meaning trans women. It is important to keep that in mind as we navigate the topic of "pussy power".

As commentator and video essayist Khadija Mbowe has explained, women in rap have appropriated pussy power in a way that highlights desirability and the power they get from it.[81] The song and music video for "WAP" (which stands for "Wet Ass Pussy") by Cardi B and Megan Thee Stallion, that became an online sensation, contains these lines:

Now get your boots and your coat for this wet ass pussy
He bought a phone just for pictures of this wet ass pussy
Pay my tuition just to kiss me on this wet ass pussy
Now make it rain if you wanna see some wet ass pussy

The song is all about pussy power and how women can get what they want from it: a car, boots, a coat, a university degree. Cardi B and Megan Thee Stallion self-objectify as a way to gain money, independence and therefore power. In the lyrics, they associate "pussy power" and desirability with materialism and wealth. As Tee Noir described in a video essay on the topic, the typical Black female rapper is "confident", "intriguing", "fearless and tirelessly defends her position in the hypersexual market. […] Language is her most powerful weapon."[82] Black female rappers have reclaimed the hypersexual stereotype that has historically been assigned to them and attached capitalist opulence to it. Knowing that sociologists have, until recently, called Black communities in poor areas "the underclass" living in a "culture of poverty",[83] imagine how empowering it must feel to use the codes of that "culture of poverty" and make millions out of it.

Male rappers have been doing it for decades now and female rappers have only recently caught up. Black men rap about the social status sex gives them. Black women, on the other hand, rap about the economic status "the pussy" (something that, Tee Noir noted, is detached from the human being) gives them, and it has been a bit of a revolution. The hip-hop industry is now dominated by female artists. Conservative politicians and commentators' constant criticism of female rappers' music videos and lyrics is symptomatic of their success. However, sex — as an emancipating and pleasurable act — is almost systematically disregarded for status. What is liberating for Cardi B isn't the sexual act, but what sex as a currency can afford her. This is obviously not limited to Black female rappers, as hip-hop culture has been appropriated outside the Black community, but their unapologetic reclamation of hypersexuality makes them an interesting case study.

Nevertheless, as soon as female rappers reach a certain level of financial status and fame, they start to distance themselves from hypersexuality.[84] Specifically, the hypersexual character of the lyrics and video performances is counterbalanced by a discourse that rather aligns with purity culture. In an interview with *Elle Magazine*, Nicki Minaj declared she was going to go in the opposite direction and hope her then-new album *Queen* would show women that it's "okay to keep your legs closed".[85] In a — maybe ironic, maybe not so ironic — way, Megan Thee Stallion said she preferred to keep her body count low on Hot97's *Ebro in the Morning*.[86] In "My Type", Saweetie, who is often seen wearing sex workers' Pleaser shoes, raps that "You the type that's fuckin' for the rent (You a thot)".[87] As Khadija Mbowe noted, icons like Beyoncé and Megan Thee Stallion, but also Arianna Grande, Dua Lipa, Madonna and many others, can perform hypersexuality, adopt sex workers' aesthetic and still remain safe. They can capitalise on hypersexuality with the knowledge that someone will drive them home to their gated communities.[88] Only women who are desirable, safe and whose bank account is so secured that they don't have to care about reputation can truly benefit from "pussy power", and still, it is not something they brag about outside the context of their job.

That is why romanticising "pussy power" into something inherently liberating for women is, in my opinion, limiting. To paraphrase Mbowe, desirability — in this case pussy power — is a trap.[89] Behind "WAP"'s glossy music video is the story of a woman who chose sex work to escape violence and poverty and go back to school.[90] Her story echoes that of young working-class people who choose sex work to become financially secure, support themselves through college or pay off debt.

With the internet, new forms of sex work have emerged. "Sugar-babying" is arguably one of them. I remember watching niche documentaries ten years ago in which sugar babies secretly filmed dates with potential sugar daddies and revealed how dangerous and exploitative sugar babying is. These documentaries have now been replaced by a different type of content. On social media like TikTok, Instagram and YouTube, spoiled sugar babies share all the gifts, travels and five-figure monthly allowances they receive from their sugar daddies. The song "Sugar Daddy" by Qveen Herby (who has probably never had a sugar daddy) served as a template for the TikTok trend:

He love me, he give me all his money
That Gucci, Prada comfy
My sugar daddy

As these lyrics unfold, the sugar baby reveals a picture of her and her sugar daddy with their respective ages (gaps generally range from thirty to fifty years), followed by a selection of the shoes, bags and holidays he has given her. As I was going through the videos, I noticed that the sugar daddy always looked the same: a tall, rather fit man with a beard and grey hair, a George Clooney clone, to be honest. It is important to note that the sugar baby can also be a man or a non-binary person, the sugar daddy can be a mommy, and the relationship doesn't have to be heterosexual. Nevertheless, most sugar babies are young women between the ages of eighteen and twenty-five.

While it is often glamorised online as a lifestyle, sugar babying must be understood as employment with its specific risks, obligations and rights. Risks, because not all sugar daddies look like a George Clooney clone who respects consent and boundaries; obligations, because the sugar baby enters a contractual relationship where she is expected to provide a certain number of services in exchange of money and products; rights (and that is where things get tricky) because, like any worker, she deserves to be protected by the law. Unfortunately, sugar babies are in an ambivalent situation where they operate under the construct of a relationship, not a business. Clients technically pay for the company of the sugar baby, but the line between company and intimacy is often blurred. The "relationship" label is what prevents sugar babies from being labelled as sex workers, which would make sugar-babying illegal in many countries. In other words, sugar babies are forced to accept the flexible "relationship" label to prevent sugar daddies from facing retribution. Some sugar babies do create what looks like a normal relationship with their respective sugar daddy/mommy, one that involves feelings and reciprocity. Many have shared that they felt like their companionship helped sugar daddies feel cared for and less lonely. However, it is crucial not to glamorise a practice that — at the moment and because it is not regulated — attracts people who are financially unstable and most likely to remain powerless in the face of exploitation or violence.[91] It is also essential to understand sugar-babying as part of the gig economy, meaning that the seemingly entrepreneurial nature of the job only serves to increase the margins made by those leading the industry. Like gig economy workers, sugar babies are not incentivised to organise themselves in unions because they remain in the industry for a limited amount of time. Nevertheless, they remain, for the majority, working-class workers exploited by an unjust system.

On TikTok, sugar babies are often asked which websites they use to find their sugar daddy. SugarDaddy.com and SeekingArrangement.com seem to be among the most popular. Seeking Arrangement dominated the market until it turned into a regular dating website. Its founder and CEO

Brandon Wade created it in 2006 and has made millions out of it. He therefore scaled his business for more specific demands with MissTravel.com, meant to pair rich travellers with young attractive women, and OpenMinded.com for open relationships. Wade is considered by many as an e-pimp, he owes his wealth to the young women who are on his websites and make his businesses grow. The fifty-one-year-old millionaire now enjoys a life of luxury with his now "21-year-old soulmate"[92] while his workers are prey to exploitation and abuse.

OnlyFans, founded by yet another man, Timothy Stokely, in 2016, appears to many as a safer option when compared to sugar-babying. Made to look like a traditional social media platform, people posting on OnlyFans are called "content creators". Like YouTube (45%) or Twitch (50%), OnlyFans takes a percentage of the subscriptions and ad revenue generated by its creators (20%, a relatively low percentage, which they love to promote as part of their red-washing strategy). The difference between sugar-babying and OnlyFans is that the first one is based on a time-for-money transaction, whereas the second one provides content that can be viewed by an unlimited number of people 24/7. That is precisely why creators like Cardi B, Bella Thorne, Safaree Samuels and others can make millions every month on the platform. As we saw earlier with the street interviews, OnlyFans is what comes to people's minds when they are asked about "pussy power". The creators have full control over the content they produce, and they do not engage in direct physical contact with their clients, which makes their work safer. Many say that OnlyFans has revolutionised sex work by providing safety and financial stability to its creators, and to be frank, such a statement is hardly refutable. It almost legitimises what the

street interviewer said, namely that pussy privilege is real…
Well, not really, and here's why.

On October 15, 2022, Amouranth, one of the top-performing
female streamers and an OnlyFans star, appeared on Twitch as
usual. However, things did not go as usual. The stream stopped
at some point. Amouranth reappeared later and confessed that
she was married to an abusive husband who forced her to stream
every day and pretend she is single, controlled her finances,
and threatened to kill her dogs if she didn't complete a twenty-
four-hour livestream. She shared abusive text messages, and
was on the phone with him live while he went into a tantrum
and brought her to tears. In the meantime, the chat was out
of control. People called her a liar. They said she deserved it.
Others shamelessly used the opportunity to comfort her and say
they would take care of her and treat her well. Despite being
an institution on Twitch, and a "strong, independent woman",[93]
said streamer HasanAbi, Amouranth's image was controlled by
an exploitative and violent man.

Andrew Tate, who has been mentioned several times
already, started building his wealth by creating a webcam
business (similar to what can be done on OnlyFans) where
he forced his six girlfriends to chat with men in exchange for
money. In fact, Tate was the one chatting with men in the
live chat. He claimed he generated around $3,000 per day
with this method and ended up working with up to seventy-
five women. Realising that he was not making as much
money as he wanted, since he had to redistribute it with the
girls, he downsized to eight women, four of whom were his
girlfriends, and the other four were his brother's girlfriends.
The fact that these women were allegedly "in love with him"
allowed him to only give them 20% of the money they made,
which left $400,000 a month for him to enjoy.[94] So even if

the online format of platforms like OnlyFans and live chat webcam businesses generally protects creators from clients' abuse, we cannot be sure about what happens behind the scenes. A woman's desirability is only a privilege when she has full ownership over her content. Unfortunately, like most gig economy jobs, a platform, a man, a partner, acts as an intermediary between the creator and the client.

In *My Body*, Emily Ratajkowski wrote about the time she was invited by her boyfriend's friend to Richard Prince's *Instagram Paintings* show. She was deceived when she realised the paintings were just printed canvases of Instagram posts, on which the artist had commented from his account.[95] One of the posts was her's. She wrote that it felt strange that a big-time, fancy artist worth a lot more money than her should be able to snatch one of her Instagram posts and sell it as his own.[96] In the book, she also shared that she had been sexually assaulted by photographer Jonathan Leder, who had the audacity to later publish a book titled *Ratajkowski* in which he exposed the polaroids he had taken of her both in lingerie and fully naked at his house. Ratajkowski didn't receive any compensation for the book, nor for the photoshoot she did with him; she was paid in exposure. In a Q&A session with her, philosopher Amia Srinivasan wondered how a model can assert power and control in industries that are dominated by men who "direct, film, and manage [...] who own the companies and production houses, and who so often treat you as fungible and stupid, simply a body to be sold, consumed, and unfortunately occasionally assaulted".[97]

To conclude, it is crucial to point out that "pussy power" might increase one's financial status, but it decreases one's social status. When a woman uses her sex appeal to elevate herself, she is generally perceived as morally bad. The religiously-infused Victorian archetype of the "fallen woman" is alive and kicking. A woman who has a high body count or exposes her body online is deemed promiscuous, dirty and unfit for marriage. She is less than a human being, she becomes a rightful victim. I mean, look at the backlash Emily Ratajkowski and other celebrities received after they accused men of sexual harassment during and after #MeToo. The implication was that women who sell their image, whether they are actresses, models, performers or influencers, either deserved it, or should have known it was bound to happen. "What were you wearing?" asked students at the University of Kansas to eighteen women who had been raped. They gave them the clothes they were wearing on that day and those were exposed as part of an exhibition. Most of the outfits were not "sexy" or "provocative".

Instead of shaming women who, it is presumed, slept their way to the top, why don't we question why powerful men give more opportunities to women who sexually gratify them?[98] Why is there such an expectation in the first place? As you probably understand by now, I strongly disagree with the street interviewer I introduced at the beginning of this section. There is no such thing as "pussy privilege".

Throughout this chapter on the will *not* to change, we saw how the world of self-help (the manosphere, hardcore self-help, alternative self-help) has responded to men's struggle to find meaning by putting the blame on women. To justify their refusal to change, men have accused society of pathologizing masculinity; they came up with a concept like "pussy privilege", which supposes that women hold more power than men. On the other hand, those who *have* the will to change are prey to discourses that promote a return to essentialist modes of being meant to realign individuals with the universal laws of nature.

They are stuck somewhere on a spectrum from toxic to healthy masculinity that can prevent them from experimenting beyond the boundaries of a fixed gender expression. In conclusion, having the will to change shouldn't be limited to changes in individual behaviours. It should be channelled into the (love) revolution against the neoliberal heterosexual institution that isolates us in oppressive structures.

Chapter 2
Making Society Pure Again

A Return to Purity Culture?

On July 11, 2017, at 3.19am, Cole LaBrant tweeted "No longer a virgin #MarriageRocks".[1]

Cole LaBrant is the father of a super popular vlogging family. His pride in announcing that he was no longer a virgin (probably right after it happened, which makes the tweet even more... peculiar) is indicative of the value put on sexual abstinence. Likewise, YouTuber Jouelzy remembered a group of girls at her university who cheerfully bragged about their virginity, turning purity into a social currency.[2]

The commodification of virginity as a social currency is as old as time. During the Middle Ages, affluent families sought to preserve their daughters' chastity to ensure a good, profitable marriage. Whether the family paid for the union, or the future husband did, the virginity of the adolescent woman was to be kept. Controlling a girl's sexuality was a way for the family to prevent seduction, impregnation or paternity claims on a child during the process of finding the right suitor. The suitor, on the other hand, often sought upward mobility through marriage. It was, and remains, a common theme of European/Western fairytales. As anthropologist Alice Schlegel noted, the "poor but honest man goes through trials to win the hand of the princess".[3] The princess's purity is what makes her worthy of such efforts.

The early commodification of virginity meant that it was almost perceived as a product within a woman's body that could be extracted from her or restored. For instance, Countess Elizabeth Bàthory of Hungary wanted to recapture her youth and alleged beauty after her husband died. An alchemy enthusiast, she read that bathing in the blood of virgins could help her in her quest, and so she did. She killed approximately six hundred virgins who worked for her or were sent to her finishing school.[4] Flashforward to 1974, when *Jet Mag* published an issue in which one could find a "virginity diet". It did not consist of virgin blood this time, but rather a combination of "asparagus, orange, lemon juice, eggs and honey". It advised to "drink only in the morning in bed, alone".[5]

Today, the commodification of virginity fosters the exploitation and assault of adolescent women across the globe. It was revealed that Peru's gold miners sought "good luck" by raping trafficked virgin girls sold by their parents or relatives based on false promises of making them domestics.[6] The girls get auctioned off to clients in North America, Mexico, Japan and other industrialised countries. Virginity tests and genital mutilation are also still widely practiced in many countries across the globe despite efforts to make it illegal.[7] Finally, young women capitalise on their virginity for upward mobility. A Brazilian student auctioned her virginity for £485,000[8], an American med student did the same for $800,000,[9] as did a British student who needed to pay for her mother's debts and start her business.[10]

Now, why are men willing to pay huge amounts of money to take away a young woman's virginity? Why is it so valuable? What does it say about the way we view female sexuality?

To answer this question, we can first look at what happened in Iran in 2022. The leaders of the Islamic revolution, many in their eighties, decided that the control of female sexuality or female sexual appeal through the imposition of the hijab was necessary to ensure the Islamic society is purified.[11] By "purified", they mean that heterosexual men aren't sexually aroused by women in public. Because of that, Iranian women are policed by everyone in the public space. Men regularly harass partly-veiled or unveiled women in the streets, as we glimpsed in the numerous videos that were shared on social media. The Iranian situation is reminiscent of the way Vestals were treated in Ancient Rome. Vestals' purity was sought to ensure the purity of Roman society. Vestals ought to remain virgins and those who engaged in sexual relationships were condemned for treason and buried alive in the city.[12] In Iran, Mahsa Amini, who went out in public partly veiled, was said to have been tortured and killed by the morality police. What happened in Iran has triggered a lot of debates on the different ways in which modesty can be imposed or chosen. In fact, while modesty is synonymous with oppression for a lot of Iranian women, Western women's choice of modesty is rather defined (by those who are vocal about it) as a form of liberation.

In May 2021, *Vogue* revealed some of the pictures they took of Billie Eilish alongside bits of a much-anticipated interview. The pictures went viral because it was the first time Eilish had ditched the baggy clothes for a bombshell outfit centred around a pastel pink corset. Her message was the following: "It's all about what makes you feel good". Unsurprisingly, popular conservative commentators were very disappointed to see that. Billie Eilish's (modest) baggy clothing and critique of porn had attracted conservatives' sympathy. However, she had suddenly changed her mind and now encouraged women to dress like "prostitutes", according to Steven Crowder.[13] Eilish has been vocal in multiple interviews about the reason why she often wears baggy clothes. Specifically, she prefers to hide what's underneath so that nobody can have an opinion on her. People simply don't know; they can only speculate.[14] So, modesty for her means that she protects herself from unwanted comments on her physique.

In a tweet posted in October 2022, popular French twitch streamer Maghla shared what it's like to be a female content creator. She told her followers that she often changes her outfit before going live, switching from close-fitting to baggy looks, because she doesn't want to have to deal with remarks. She then detailed the type of sexual harassment she faces on Reddit, Discord, in forums and in direct messages. Dick pics, comments on how she's going to be raped, pictures of herself with sperm on and pictures of herself superposed on porn actresses, can all be found on the internet or in her DMs. As a content creator myself, I regularly receive comments from people who want to police the way I dress on camera. One adult man once said, "I liked the video but the top is too riskay so I won't share it". I was wearing a black tank top and a cardigan that left one shoulder bare.

The regulation of female sexuality online through sexual harassment, as well as its exploitation through monetised content like social commentaries or non-consensual deepfake porn,[15] has forced female influencers to choose modesty in order to work freely.

Finally, in an article she published in 2008, Naomi Wolf

showed how a Western Muslim woman related modesty to freedom:

> When I wear Western clothes, men stare at me, objectify me, or I am always measuring myself against the standards of models in magazines, which are hard to live up to — and even harder as you get older, not to mention how tiring it can be to be on display all the time. When I wear my headscarf or *chador*, people relate to me as an individual, not an object; I feel respected.[16]

This woman wanted to be perceived as a human being, not a sexual object. She took it upon herself to cancel her gender signifiers and become neutral to the eyes of others. Now, women's ability to choose how to dress in public is the business of nobody but themselves. Fighting for the ability to choose, like French Muslim women continuously do in France with the hijab, is empowering. If women feel more comfortable in public wearing the headscarf or baggy clothes, it is their right to do so. However, the liberal press's glorification of women who choose to remain modest prevents us from addressing the roots of the problem — the male gaze. Modesty cannot be the answer to the sexualisation of women's bodies. We must question why female is sexual and male is neutral. Going back to Wolf's article, I found it interesting that she later referred to that sexualising gaze she and the Muslim woman felt as the "Western gaze".[17] When Wolf writes about having "the curve of [her] breasts covered, the shape of [her] legs obscured, [her] long hair not flying about [her]",[18] the reader immediately understands who she's specifically hiding from — men. She reported feeling free, and I'll argue she felt free from the male gaze, not the Western gaze, since she precisely described how men sexualise women in the street.

Wolf's stance on modesty is characteristic of 2000s-2010s liberal feminism, which uncritically worshiped choice. Since then, scholars, feminists, journalists and content creators have brought a bit of nuance to choice feminism by delving into the concept of the "male gaze" and how women internalise it. The term was coined in 1975 by film critic Laura Mulvey to refer to the representation of women in visual arts and literature from a male, heterosexual perspective. The popularity of this topic on social media is proof of how people, especially women, find it relevant. In 2021, TikTok turned it into a recognisable trend using the hashtag #writtenbyaman. Creators filmed themselves studying with a high-ponytail, playing with a pen in their mouth; reading a book in lingerie lying in bed with a glass of wine; changing into their pyjamas as if they were doing a strip-tease; dancing like a stripper in the morning as they prepare breakfast, spilling water on their shirt as they drink; in the office playing with their hair, their back exaggeratedly arched. Comedian Caitlin Riley became internet famous with a series of videos she titled "How Women Are Written in Sci-Fi Movies/War Movies/Action Movies" where female characters are reduced to the emotional mother, damsel in distress or *femme fatale* stereotypes. I personally found the trend both hilarious and comforting. It felt like someone finally materialised something women have felt for ages, and there is no better way to do that than through humour.

Aside from the funny videos, video essayists, commentators and journalists further educated their audience on the ways in which the male gaze is internalised and exercised unconsciously. The conversation on female sexualisation therefore evolved from Wolf's "women are inherently sexual", which ultimately puts the blame on women for having breasts, hips, legs and hair, to "women are inherently sexualised", which displaces responsibility onto what sexualises — the male gaze. It also led a growing number of women to reject the male gaze and adopt an aesthetic that, like Billie Eilish, makes them feel comfortable, no matter how "unattractive" on the one hand or "sexualising" on the other it may be. A woman once commented under one of my videos that she stopped looking at herself as an inherently sexual being and chose instead to adopt a body neutrality approach. She shared that, progressively, she felt better in her body, stopped comparing herself to others and naturally stopped seeing everything as sexual.

In fact, conservative political commentator Steven Crowder may criticise Billie Eilish for wearing a corset that reveals her large breasts, but he regularly wears a retro pistol holster around his shoulders defining his manly chest. In both cases, they perform femininity or masculinity with clothes and accessories that highlight certain features, but only Eilish is called out for it. She is called out for it because, as a cultural icon, her display of sexual appeal is perceived as representative of the state of depravity Western societies are in. As is the case in most conservative regimes, the level of regulation of female sexuality serves as a metric to evaluate the purity of a culture.

"Conservatives Are Bad at Sex"[19]

Eros is irrelevant, conservatives say. Left-wing social conservatives tend to see it as a bourgeois notion. *Eros* is prey to capitalism because the pleasurable emotions stemming from *eros*, passionate love and lust, can easily be commodified into what Illouz called "emodities".[20] Communist Slavoj Žižek talked of erotic love as a catastrophe.[21] Communist Michael Hardt said it is wrong to believe the sexual revolution was a social revolution. Journalist and activist Ece Temelkuran says *eros* is a frozen topic.[22] The only form of love worthy of scientific and political attention for them is *agápē*, communal love. They are right that sexuality is primarily about the self, and sure, to paraphrase philosopher Leslie Green, it doesn't have to be spiritual, political or intellectual; it can just be hot, wet or fun.[23] In fact, a song like "WAP" doesn't have to be emancipatory or politically relevant to be enjoyable. Interestingly, the people who listen to Cardi B or Megan Thee Stallion are mostly women and queer people. However, we must be conscious that hypersexual music feeds a thirst for power more than a thirst for intimacy. Mistaking one for the other is proof that we have work to do, taboos to remove, and that means we must take sex/*eros* seriously — which in my vocabulary means the-personal-is-politicising it. If we refuse to do that work, it means we leave it for others to profit from.

The sexual liberation movement of the 1960s made sex positivity trendy to the point where conservatives were forced to jump on the bandwagon. In *The Act of Marriage: The Beauty of Sexual Love*, Beverly LaHaye, who founded the conservative organisation Concerned Women for America in 1979, and her husband Tim offered to improve Christians' sex lives. The book was a bestseller, with more than 2.5 million copies sold. It gave practical insights on what a fulfilling sex life can look like, all supported by Bible passages and therefore approved by God. The LaHayes were dedicated to the conservative cause and the book perfectly fit with their objective as Christian activists. In fact, Tim LaHaye was the founder and president of Family Life seminars, a national family ministry that organised conferences throughout the country. With *The Act of Marriage*, which is said to have saved hundreds of marriages, the conservative couple ensured that families did not break apart at a time where no-fault divorces were becoming more socially accepted.

Today, the YouTube sisters Kristen and Bethany Beal, on their channel *girldefined*, follow the path set by the LaHayes by providing a safe space for discussions on Christian sexuality. The sisters want to shed light on issues that are seldom discussed in Christian circles, for example how to deal with lustful thoughts. In their book *Sex, Purity, and the Longings of a Girl's Heart*, the sisters talk about their struggles wrestling with the urge to masturbate and societal pressures to have sex outside of marriage. Quoting passages from the Bible, they encourage girls to align themselves with God's intentions regarding sexuality, which means no sex before marriage and no lustful thoughts. However, since writing the book, Bethany has got married and now seeks to challenge purity culture and bring back sex positivity to conservatism. In an Instagram reel she posted in November 2021, her husband is seen putting whipped cream into her mouth as she joyfully rolls her shoulders and looks up to him over Taylor Swift's "… Ready For It?". "Keeping things fun and spicy" was included in the caption. It is understandable that the *girldefined* sisters and female conservative influencers in general want to educate Christian women on what sex is like. However, the rapid shift from "don't consume anything remotely sexual" to "here's the new vibrator I got" can be confusing to their audience.[24] Newly married conservatives promoting liberated, spicy sex after years and years of sexual repression sounds and looks forced. In fact, Bethany Beal's sex positive transformation received a good amount of criticism from Christians who thought she was going too far. My goal isn't to establish whether conservatives are allowed to experiment with sexuality, but to figure out if anyone should listen to their advice.

As someone who is not religious, it is interesting to see how interpretations of the same Bible passages vary according to different Christians. To the question of "Is Oral Sex a Sin in Marriage?", Christian content creators Dave and Ashley Willis answered by looking into "the best marriage book", the Bible, in which they did not find anything restricting oral sex. Also, during an episode of their *XO Marriage* podcast, Ashley argued that vibrators are desensitising women in a way that prevents them from reaching orgasm with their male partner. The vibrations provided by the sex toy cannot be reproduced by the male's genitalia, she said, or normal intercourse, her husband added. As a matter of fact, Tristan Tate, the infamous brother of the infamous manosphere star Andrew Tate, tweeted something similar:

> Unpopular opinion — there is a physical difference in sex with women who have never used sex toys. Blasting your vagina with battery powered gizmos has a physical effect and men can tell. I don't care who this offends.

In all honesty, this argument has become a go-to for men who cannot give pleasure to women and women who feel bad for them.

Right-wing political commentator Ben Shapiro's assessment of the music video for "WAP" by Cardi B and Megan Thee Stallion is probably one of the most tragic moments in the history of online conservatives and sex. Convinced that the two female rappers' vaginal lubrication was symptomatic of a medical condition, Shapiro recommended they see a gynaecologist. In doing so, he portrayed himself as someone who has never sexually aroused a woman. Implicitly admitting his incompetence, reactionary influencer Andrew Tate has often bragged that he doesn't care about the female orgasm. He has described sex as boring and enjoyed being violent with his partners.[25] Myron Gaines of the *Fresh and Fit* podcast (which, just to remind you, claims to provide the "truth on females") said on an episode that female orgasm is useless.[26] Rollo Tomassi, who was invited onto another episode and is known for being the founder of the redpill community, also said that women tend to fake more with dominant, alpha men because they expect betas to do the extra work and get them to orgasm.[27] Gaines used Tomassi's "observation" to tell his male audience to become more dominant, so that they don't have to care about their partner's reaching orgasm, I guess.

Now, here's the final reason why you should not listen to conservatives' advice on sex. In September 2022, Peter Thiel (who invests in a variety of conservative organisations, projects and businesses) funded and released the dating app The Right Stuff. The Right Stuff only caters to heterosexual audiences and soon had to wrestle with a major problem: an absence of female users. One user complaint read as follows:

> These days, it's hard to find a woman who values my patriotism. My faith. And so after being ghosted by every match on Tinder, I decided to give this app a try. [...] But the weird thing was, I couldn't find any women on it. I don't know, maybe the app is bugged?[28]

Thiel might have overestimated women's enthusiasm for conservative men. The *truth* provided by pick-up artists like the hosts of the *Fresh and Fit* podcast, Andrew Tate, redpillers and conservatives may not be true in practice.

On the other hand, progressives — more specifically the LGBTQ+ and feminist movements — have always fought to spread sexual literacy so that we can *all* have fun. In a big-sister-energy type of video, Jouelzy encouraged her viewers (the #SmartBrownGirl, as she calls them) to discover themselves as centres of pleasure.[29] Still in the Black content creation sphere, F.D. Signifier turned his channel into a space for open, informed conversations on Black love and sexuality. In video deep dives connecting the personal and the political, he invites young men to "untake" the red pill and deprogram themselves from the manosphere.

These individuals re-politicise self-help or *self-health* through education and consciousness-raising. A few years ago, I had the chance to interview Norma Mtume, an activist who was very active in the West Coast free health clinics of the Black Panther Party for Self-Defense in the late 1960s. The clinics were the place where the Black community developed a system of self-health for self-defence against the racist state. The Panthers involved in the clinics educated themselves with the help of doctors, medical students, nurses and "a lot of reading" to then educate their patients in return. Ultimately, the goal was to forge strong bodies ready for the revolution the leaders of the movement were aiming for. Through education, prevention and care, volunteers turned their patients into actors of their own health. They were then able to defend themselves against both the physical violence and the symbolic violence of the state and fight for equal rights. In other words, *self-health* became political.[30]

Mtume shared that they had to do a lot of prevention regarding AIDS and other sexual diseases. During our interview, she mentioned the book *Our Bodies, Ourselves*, which she said she recommended and gifted to girls and teenagers.

The book, written by the Boston's Women's Health Book Collective, was first published in 1973. Taking a self-health approach, the twelve college-educated women that formed the collective decided to write an extremely accessible booklet where they would compile, with the help of professionals, everything they had learned from their own research.[31] It revolutionised women's lives as it removed the taboo from topics like sexual health, sexual orientation, orgasm, gender identity, birth control, abortion, pregnancy, etc. The strength of the book is that it centred on the power of education, solidarity and acceptance, which are all part of the process of consciousness-raising. It spread knowledge to individuals who were denied the right to *really* know, or at least weren't incentivised to.

These online Black feminists and activists follow the legacy of people like Norma Mtume, or the women behind *Our Bodies, Ourselves*. They offer radical perspectives on love and sexuality. Taking a critical look at how capitalist modes of consumption have penetrated our sexual and love life, they seek to redefine what those terms really mean and in doing so, assert that *eros*, passionate love, can be liberating.

Back to the Family

When social conservatives go on long nostalgic monologues ranting about how life was wonderful "before" (the "before" is never clearly defined), they romanticise what they believe used to be a purer, more traditional society. Before, men would conduct themselves in a way that would make them worthy husbands to pure, non-promiscuous wives. The control of young men was operated through the control of the sexuality of adolescent and young adult women, conditioned by religious morality. That's why virtually all social conservatives see the sexual revolution as a failure. When talking about the contraceptive pill, journalist Louise Perry argued that "when motherhood became a biological choice for women, fatherhood became a social choice for men".[32] By that she means that a woman's ability to choose whether she wants babies was answered by the man's ability to choose whether to abandon his father's duties.[33]

Perry is part a new brand of self-proclaimed common-sense feminists that has gained popularity on social media. She is the author of *The Case Against the Sexual Revolution: A New Guide to Sex in the 21st Century*, which, according to *Guardian* journalist Rachel Cooke, "may turn out to be one of the most important feminist books of its time".[34] Perry has been successful at cultivating her ambiguity. She is a *New Statesman* columnist, where she has written on drag shows, social media influencers, survivalists, family life, maternity leave and *Roe v. Wade*. Every time she writes or speaks publicly, she remains tolerant enough to keep her feminist label, but also cultivates among her readers a strong anti-liberal-elite, pro-family sentiment. In fact, during an interview for the *Spectator*, interviewer Fraser Nelson was confused as to why a *New Statesman* journalist would write a book promoting family values.[35] The hybridity of Perry and other common-sense feminists allows them to convey their conservative political message across the political spectrum.

To be honest, I was dismayed to see the *Guardian*, a liberal media outlet, share such a positive review of Perry's book. The writer Rachel Cooke did not agree with everything Perry had to say, especially her chapter on marriage (which is conveniently positioned at the end of the book, after the consensual anti-hook-up-culture sections). Disagreeing with the conclusion of a book, and therefore its thesis, should translate into a negative or at least nuanced review but no, *The Case Against the Sexual Revolution* is "one of the most important feminist books of its time".

It is important to take Perry's opinion on marriage and family seriously, because first, it is dangerously regressive, and second, I strongly suspect we will see more "common-sense" feminists like her in the future. Indeed, Perry's appearances on conservative and liberal social media platforms have attracted a lot of attention and millions of views. So, I suspect that in the same way Jordan B. Peterson became the self-help guru of a generation of young men in search of meaning, traditional common-sense feminists like Perry could influence a generation of young women who feel the same way.

In the *Spectator* interview, subtitled "Fraser Nelson speaks to Louise Perry [...] about why more people should be getting married, and why it should be harder to get divorced", Perry looked back on the Divorce Reform Act of 1969 as a marker of the beginning of a new era she cannot help but badly connote — the post-sexual-revolution era. The act was revolutionary because it enabled partners to file for "no-fault" divorce. After 1969, divorce rates increased tremendously as unhappy couples were finally allowed to legally end their marriage.[36] But what about the children?, asks Perry. In all truth, every attack on the nuclear family, whether it's related to women's rights, LGBTQ+ rights, trans rights, etc., is met with some conservatives claiming that "we must save our children". Interestingly, those same conservatives systematically relegate family support to the private sphere. But Perry is a common-sense *feminist*, she knows how to differentiate herself from hardcore conservatives. For instance, she supports several pro-family welfare measures, including the improvement of maternity leave. In a podcast interview with Mikhaila Peterson, she said she was about to go to a weekend event put on by a conservative thinktank that would provide childcare so that mothers could join carefree. She rightly highlighted that feminist organisations used to provide similar services during conferences.[37] This is an interesting point of connection between a pro-family (supposedly right-wing) and pro-social (supposedly left-wing) political agenda that we need to be careful about.

Natality is decreasing all over the world, nationalism is on the rise and reactionaries talk about "the great replacement", meaning that white, Western populations are being demographically and culturally replaced with non-white populations. Therefore, incentives to encourage specific groups of women to have children and support them in that process need to be taken with a grain of salt. For instance, Vladimir Putin's government decided to rehabilitate the Soviet Union "Mother Heroine" title, which offers a hero's medal and $16,000 to women who have ten kids.[38] Similarly, French far-right candidate Éric Zemmour promised he would give €10,000 "for every child born in a rural family" during the 2022 presidential campaign.[39] Marine Le Pen, who isn't known for supporting women's rights but won more than 40% of the French vote in 2022, has started imposing the topic of natality in debates, and has inspired the traditional right-wing party to do the same.[40]

Perry claims that being a stay-at-home mother isn't as easy as it used to be — "you won't have the social support that you used to have".[41] She must be oblivious to the fact that we have progressively moved towards greater social support for families, including mothers. Progress is rather slow, one might argue, and countries like the US are far behind what is provided in Europe, but it is false to argue that mothers had more support in the past. What Perry may be referring to however is something like the Fordist family wage in the US, which "assigned unionised men the waged role in productive labour and white women an unpaid role as domestic workers in the household".[42] According to sociologist Melinda Cooper, the Fordist family wage is a good example of capitalism's preservation of the family. This form of welfarism continued up till Nixon's second presidency with the Family Assistance Plan. However, support for the welfare rights movement stopped during Nixon's second term. Neoliberal advocates of the extension of family support — including Milton Friedman and Daniel Patrick Moynihan — realised that welfare was also distributed to people who made non-traditional lifestyle choices and they didn't like it.[43]

To Perry, traditional living and religiosity are sources of inspiration. In their review of *The Case Against the Sexual Revolution*, *The Gospel Coalition* noticed that the list of chapter titles, including "Sex Must Be Taken seriously" (chap. 1), "Men and Women Are Different" (chap. 2), "Some Desires Are Bad" (chap. 3), "almost sounds like a preaching series based on the opening chapters of Genesis".[44]

What is wrong with taking inspiration from the Bible?, some will ask. Well, I could redirect you to the previous section on conservatives and sex, but I'll simply say that the Bible is a very old, patriarchal text. In fact, Christian feminist scholars denounce the privileged perspective used in the way beliefs and practices are recorded and interpreted which makes it difficult for people at the margins to be heard.[45] Using the Bible as a source of inspiration for how to interact with each other — in our case through committed and non-committed relationships — necessitates that the author (especially one that claims to be a feminist) lends a critical eye to the text. Perry does not do so. She ends the book with chapters titled "Marriage is Good" and "Listen to Your Mother". The tone is very paternalistic. It reproduces the verticality of a text like the Bible. Looking backward for answers is, for me, not a good idea. An inclusive, non-paternalistic approach to finding solutions is one that is horizontal, that is chosen by people because it makes sense at that specific moment.

To conclude this part on whether sexual liberation was a failure, I agree that the co-optation of sexual liberation by the patriarchal-capitalist system (meaning that an active sex life enhances one's social/economic status) has prompted young people to choose to be sexually active when they didn't really know if they wanted to. However, this view of sexual liberation reduces the very concept of liberation to the act of transgression. As we have seen throughout this second part, discussions on sexuality for the sake of sexuality are rare, taboo. The way we approach this topic as a society, notably through sex education, is rather conservative. While there has been in the second half of the twentieth century a liberation of people's attitude towards sex, the discourse around it hasn't changed much. The sexual liberation we talk about today still revolves around the idea of a transgression of norms. In other words, our bodies and sexuality are still surveilled and therefore regulated.[46]

Conclusion

Rethinking Work

In Part I, we saw how the downfall of the girlboss left us with a daunting question: What happens when work is no longer synonymous with liberation?

We have failed to translate online movements like "I don't dream of labor", "quiet-quitting" and more generally speaking the topic of anti-work, into an alternative to the work-domesticity binary imposed on women. Because of that, domesticity — which has always been part of women's lives — now appears to signal liberation. At least, that is how traditional living advocates frame it. Leaving the capitalist workplace to embrace domesticity is turned into a subversive act and we cannot let that happen. Women were incentivised to join the workforce to participate in the economy, become financially independent and find meaning outside the home. Some privileged classes of women did benefit from their inclusion in the workplace. However, other classes of women feel overworked, exploited and unfulfilled. They don't dream of labour, they don't want to put all their energy into developing a career, some can't even afford an education or a life outside work. Now is the time to change our approach, to ditch the "bullshit jobs" and bring back meaning into work. To do that, people must work less so that they can invest time into other forms of work like housekeeping (for all, not just women), gardening, community work, volunteering, education, politicisation or leisure activities like creating art or doing sports. "Sure, a lot of it would be nonsense", said anthropologist David Graeber, "but it's hard to imagine a full 40-50% would be doing nonsense, and that's the situation we have today", he added in reference to the amount of people who think their job is "bs".[1]

Rethinking the Family

The left's campaigns against the heterosexual nuclear family, its ambiguous position on porn and its support of trans youth are used by the right — so people who generally vote to defund school breakfast programs, family benefits and childcare — to paint it as anti-family. It is time the left reclaimed the topic of the family. The first step is to redefine it. Today, the typical family is a small, private caring unit. The function of care is almost systematically relegated to its female members: the sister, the mother, the aunt, the grandmother. This structure of the family has claimed caring, sharing and loving as its own and "has made the outside world cold and friendless".[2] In order to rethink the family, one must go beyond kinship to incorporate community. One way to do that is to diversify the types of relationships we value. We mentioned in Part II the power of *agapè*, communal love, which can be exerted through friendship.[3] Friendship has been for many a refuge outside the family because the family does not always sustain itself and can repress individuality, be a place of violence or foster social and ideological isolation. Friendship, on the other hand, means openness because there are always more friends to meet, to be introduced to, and therefore new life experiences to learn from and connect with. Friendship is subversive, because those who choose to prioritise it, and in that process reject the family, are in a position of resistance. To diminish its value, deep friendship is either sexualised ("they must be gay") to materialise deviance, or reconnected to kinship (sisterhood, fraternity) to cancel the presumption of homosexuality and go back to the family.[4] It is believed that deep human connections can only be achieved through sex or romance — or the eventual product of them both, the family. That is how you end up with discourses promoting the right to sex as a cure for incels' loneliness,[5] and marriage as a cure for impersonal hook-up culture.[6] It is time for us to promote new forms of intimacy, revalorise friendship and envision the family as necessarily boundless.

Rethinking the Internet

The internet is simultaneously a space for the definition of the self and the building of communities. Throughout this book, we have seen how online communities influence the adoption of certain lifestyles, ideologies and gender expressions. We saw how, together, influencers, gurus and viewers regulate expressions of the self through surveillance. However, some sections of the internet escape the digital panopticon. For instance, VRchat, an online virtual world platform, has become "a playground of identity, anything you want to be, anything you can dream of",[7] says YouTuber Strasz. In fact, in just a few clicks, VR players can change their outfit, their accessories, their username, but also their gender. Many male players pick anime girls as their avatar so that it can allow them to "act feminine" — be vulnerable, show empathy or simply "look cute".[8] On the other hand, picking a male character implies they would need to perform peak masculinity, which is exhausting. By adopting the opposite gender characteristics for long periods of time, VRchat users can experience a balanced identification with both genders and develop less gender-stereotypical beliefs about themselves.[9] In other words, switching gender through VR changed participants' perception of gender as a fixed binary. It's not so much that VR is "woke", but rather that the internet is a space characterised by irony and performance. Like the section on fitgirls explained, VRchat users deconstruct gender unconsciously, through their own body or an extension of their body, their avatar. Other internet users who already question their gender identity — author Legacy Russell calls them *glitches*[10] — can use the built-in irony of VRchat to safely experiment and forge their individuality.

On the internet, explorations of the self are prey to the totalising presence of the online self-help industry. From the manosphere to alternative self-help, online self-help projects the aesthetic of community only to attract young people in search of meaning and willing to buy its courses and ideologies. It is time to go back to the essence of the internet, which is peer-to-peer collaboration. A platform like Wikipedia should inspire us in building this alternative. On Wikipedia, people around the world can contribute, edit and challenge articles that are accessible to everyone for free and in many different languages. None of the contributors are paid, yet this internet institution managed to completely destroy a more than two-hundred-year-old capitalist market of encyclopaedias.[11] De-privatisation is a necessary step to give the internet back to the people, for it is the people who made it — from underwater cables to the screen of your computer.[12]

De-privatisation also means that we can rethink how we recommend content online. At the moment, Big Tech platforms dictate what ends up on your social media feed based on what keeps people engaged on the platform. They exploit peer-to-peer collaboration in the form of likes, comments and shares in compliance with the demands of advertisers to determine what is relevant and what isn't. Because of that, not all user inputs are the same. I can easily predict that a video titled "Ben Shapiro DESTROYS Transgenderism and Pro-Abortion arguments" will get more views than one titled "A Brief History of the Culture Wars". In fact, I'm cheating because both videos exist on YouTube and the first one has eight times more views than the second. An educational video titled "A Brief History of Culture Wars" gets fewer views because there is nothing sensational about it. From a capitalist perspective, this video probably won't keep the user engaged on the platform as much as a sensational clickbait video. To put it simply, the left is clearly losing at the culture war game the right nurtures online. It is losing not because left-wing ideas aren't popular, but because the left doesn't lead, it catches up. We must offer something different, and create our own forms of entertainment that align with our values and are not purely reactionary.

De-privatising the internet will ensure that the production of clickbait content generated by profit-seeking individuals or bots naturally decreases. Similarly, it could incentivise online liberal and centrist media to abandon this trend of organising sensational debates on identity politics issues for the sake of engagement. Those debates claim to "show different perspectives and initiate a dialogue" but rather help to mainstream extreme ideologies, put on the same level as progressive causes through a "pro" versus "against" framework: "pro-choice vs pro-life", "flat earthers vs. scientists". Most of the time, these media don't even make the effort to fact-check what is said on their shows. I say with great seriousness that they are responsible for the standardisation of anti-feminist, anti-trans-rights and therefore anti-human-rights ideologies among younger generations.

Rethinking Society

While some look backwards for answers or indulge in apocalyptic discourses, others are determined to find solutions now and for the generations to come. Women, who have been socialised to carry with them the values of care, and minorities, who can only hope for a better future, have ambitions. We imagine a world where all forms of domination will be abolished, where humans aren't considered above nature but part of the living, where gender is an afterthought, and where the powerful tool that is the internet is a common good accessible to all. It is the duty of unapologetic radicals like us to create new narratives to shift people's consciousness and make them believe in the possibility of a better future. In 1870, Jules Verne wrote *20,000 Leagues Under the Sea*, in which he introduced the character Nemo. Nemo is an Indian man whose family was murdered by colonialists. He retaliated by appropriating and improving the technology of colonialist powers to create a model egalitarian society underwater. In other words, he became "the prototype tech-hero, turning the oppressors/dominators technology against them and repurposing it for the benefit of the rest of society", wrote Eric Hunting.[13] We can take inspiration from Nemo, but ultimately, we know that no hero will save us all. No single human being can transform society, only collectives can. Nevertheless, Nemo's prototype of an egalitarian society could become a reality. On the internet, users have popularised the imaginary of "solarpunk", which started as an art movement and aesthetic. Solarpunk is about aligning climate and social justice with how we make and build society. It is an urban aesthetic that seeks to protect all forms of living while adapting to demographic constraints.

We must train our imaginative capacities to come up with radical alternatives, but we also need to imagine how we get to materialise them. As self-help gurus tend to say: one cannot sustain a long-term vision without establishing short-term and mid-term goals. When the vision is too daunting, too unrealistic, one is more likely to give up on it. So, when thinking about a bold future, we must also think about how we get there. Social action is necessarily the answer. However, we could imagine new forms of social action that are not just reactionary — meaning that they seek to conserve previously made gains that are at risk of being lost. Instead, let's lead the fight and be bold. Let's focus our energy on younger generations and infuse hope and justice into their minds. Let's create narratives where we show young people fighting for what is *just*, where we see how radical social change gets materialised, and how communal love is forged in the process.

Notes

Preface

1   "International Women's Day: Dramatic deterioration in respect for women's rights and gender equality must be decisively reversed", *Amnesty International*, 7 March 2022, https://www.amnesty.org/en/latest/news/2022/03/international-womens-day-dramatic-deterioration-in-respect-for-womens-rights-and-gender-equality-must-be-decisively-reversed/

2   "Rapport 2023 sur l'état du sexisme en France : le sexisme perdure et ses manifestations les plus violentes s'aggravent", HCE, 2023, https://www.haut-conseil-egalite.gouv.fr/IMG/pdf/hce_-_rapport_annuel_2023_etat_du_sexisme_en_france.pdf

3   Michelle Goldberg, "The Future Isn't Female Anymore", *New York Times*, June 2022, https://www.nytimes.com/2022/06/17/opinion/roe-dobbs-abortion-feminism.html

4   Ibid.

5   A French friend of mine has created an Instagram page, @tupensesquoidufeminisme, where they share the answers they receive when they ask men, "What do you think about feminism?" on dating apps.

6   Alice Echols, *Daring to Be Bad: Radical Feminism in America, 1967-1975*, Minneapolis: University of Minnesota Press, 1989.

7   Laurence Peuron, "À gauche, le retour d›Adrien Quatennens à l›Assemblée divise les Insoumis et la Nupes", *Radio France*, 13 December 2022, https://www.radiofrance.fr/franceinter/a-

gauche-le-retour-d-adrien-quatennens-a-l-assemblee-divise-les-
insoumis-et-la-nupes-8097236

8   "If I can't dance to it, it won't be my revolution" is a sentence
     attributed to Emma Goldman after someone criticised her for
     enjoying herself as a revolutionary anarchist.

9   Ben Tarnoff, *Internet for the People*, New York: Verso Books, 2022.

10   Conversation with Donna Haraway and Marta Segarra, CCCB
     channel, Vimeo, March 2018, https://vimeo.com/258968890.

Part I: The Ideal Woman

1   Dino Felluga. "Modules on Lacan: On the Structure of the
     Psyche", *Introductory Guide to Critical Theory*, Purdue U, 31 January
     2011.

2   Jonah Peretti, "Capitalism and Schizophrenia: Contemporary
     Visual Culture and the Acceleration of Identity Formation/
     Dissolution", *Negotiations*, January 1996.

3   Richard Florida, *The Rise of the Creative Class*, New York: Basic
     Books, 2002. The concept of the creative class has been criticised
     by many, including myself in a video titled "The Failed Utopia of
     the Creative Class", https://youtu.be/PhKBBf4KGkI

4   "Suella Braverman blames 'Guardian-reading, tofu-eating
     wokerati' for disruptive protests – video", *Guardian*, 18 October
     2022, https://www.theguardian.com/politics/video/2022/
     oct/18/suella-braverman-blames-guardian-reading-tofu-eating-
     wokerati-for-disruptive-protests-video

5   Patrick Buchanan, "Culture War Speech: Address to the
     Republican National Convention", 17 August 1992, https://
     voicesofdemocracy.umd.edu/buchanan-culture-war-speech-
     speech-text/

6   @TomNicholas, "A Brief History of the Culture Wars",
     YouTube, October 2021, https://www.youtube.com/
     watch?v=TJ8ws2dqqFg

7   Vivek Ramaswamy, *Woke, Inc.*, New York: Center Street, 2021.

8 Ibid.

9 A phrase coined by Curtis Yarvin, "A Brief Explanation of the Cathedral", *Gray Mirror*, January 2021, https://graymirror. substack.com/p/a-brief-explanation-of-the-cathedral

10 Prager U, "YouTube continues to restrict many PragerU videos", https://www.prageru.com/petition/youtube

11 Todd Spangler, "Right-Wing Media Outlet Daily Wire Claims It Will Invest $100 Million in Kids' Content to Counter 'Woke' Disney Fare That Is 'Brainwashing' Children", *Variety*, 30 March 2022, https://variety.com/2022/digital/news/daily-wire-100-million-kids-entertainment-disney-1235219678/

12 @Contrapoints, "Jordan Peterson", YouTube, May 2018, https://www.youtube.com/watch?v=4LqZdkkBDas

13 Francis Dupuis-Déri, *La crise de la masculinité*, Paris : Points, 2018, p. 35-36.

14 Judith A. Allen, "Men interminably in crisis? Historians on masculinity, sexual boundaries, and manhood" *Radical History Review*, no.82, 2002.

15 @PiersMorganUncensored, "Jordan Peterson Gets Emotional Talking About Olivia Wilde's 'Incel' Comparison", YouTube, October 2022, https://www.youtube.com/watch?v=M1612L2FMHo

16 "Candace Owens on Boxing Cardi B and if Trump Should Run Again", *Full Send Podcast*, 10 February 2022.

17 Susan Faludi interviewed by Brian Lamb for C-Span, 2 October 1992, https://www.c-span.org/video/?33591-1/backlash

18 Ibid.

19 "Little Colored American", *The Colored America*, 4 October 1902.

Chapter 1: What Happens When Work Is No Longer Synonymous with Liberation?

1 Hannah Roberts, "How Giorgia Meloni thinks", *Politico Europe*, 23

September 2022, https://www.politico.eu/article/how-giorgia-meloni-thinks-brothers-of-italy-election-salvini-mario-draghi-silvio-berlusconi/?utm_source=Twitter&utm_medium=social

2   Jérôme Gautheret, Élections en Italie : qui est Giorgia Meloni, la jeune dirigeante du parti postfasciste aux portes du pouvoir?, *Le Monde*, 23 September 2022, https://www.lemonde.fr/international/article/2022/09/23/l-irresistible-ascension-de-giorgia-meloni-nouvelle-figure-de-la-droite-radicale-italienne_6142824_3210.html

3   David Broder, "Hillary Clinton Is Wrong: Electing a Far-Right Woman Is Not a Step Forward for Women", *Jacobin*, 2 September 2022, https://jacobin.com/2022/09/hillary-clinton-women-far-right-italy-giorgia-meloni-feminism

4   Angela Griuffrida, "Italy's Giorgia Meloni denies she is anti-women as credentials questioned", *Guardian*, 29 September 2022, https://www.theguardian.com/world/2022/sep/29/giorgia-meloni-italian-women-abortion-pink-quotas

5   bell hooks, *all about love: new visions*, New York: Harper, 2000.

6   Dawn Foster, *Lean Out*, London: Repeater, 2015.

7   Beate Krais, "Gender and Symbolic Violence: Female Oppression in the Light of Pierre Bourdieu's Theory of Social Practice", in Calhoun C., Lipuma E., Postone M., (eds.), *Bourdieu: Critical Perspectives*, 1993, p.156-177.

8   "Upspeak to Vocal Fry, Are We Policing Young Women's Voices?", *Fresh Air Podcast*, July 2015, https://www.npr.org/2015/07/23/425608745/from-upspeak-to-vocal-fry-are-we-policing-young-womens-voices

9   Ikuko Patricia Yuasa, "Creaky Voice: A New Feminine Voice Quality for Young Urban-Oriented Upwardly Mobile American Women?", *American Speech*, August 2010; vol. 85, no.3, p.315—337.

10   Jane Kelly, "What's in a voice? The debate over 'vocal fry' and

what it means for women", *UVA Today*, August 2015, https://news.virginia.edu/content/whats-voice-debate-over-vocal-fry-and-what-it-means-women

11 @CNBCMakeIt, "How I Sold My Start-Up To Lululemon For $500 Million", YouTube, 19 April 2021, https://www.youtube.com/watch?v=HgWoLqZILk8

12 Eve Livingston, *Make Bosses Pay: Why We Need Unions*, London: Pluto Press, 2021.

13 Eve Livingston, "The girlboss era is over, 2022 is the year of the girlunion", *i-D*, January 28, 2022, https://i-d.vice.com/en/article/5dg55k/girlboss-girlunion-era

14 Foster, *Lean Out*

15 I first saw the phrase Pastel Progressivism in Princess Weekes' video titled "Bridgerton and the Problem of Pastel Progressivism", https://www.youtube.com/watch?v=GiD_yqfqCoo

16 Michelle Goldberg, "The Future Isn't Female Anymore", *New York Times*, 17 June 2022, https://www.nytimes.com/2022/06/17/opinion/roe-dobbs-abortion-feminism.html

17 Cinzia Arruza, Tithi Bhattacharya and Nancy Fraser, *Feminism for the 99 Percent: A Manifesto*. London; New York: Verso, 2019.

18 "Sojourner Truth: Ain't I A Woman?", *National Park Service*, https://www.nps.gov/articles/sojourner-truth.htm

19 Chiara Bottici, *Anarchafeminism*, Bloomsbury Academic, London: 2021.

20 @Variety, "Kim Kardashian's Business Advice: 'Get Your F**king Ass Up and Work'", YouTube, 9 March 2022, https://www.youtube.com/watch?v=XX2izzshRmI&t=317s

21 First Nations: Land Rights and Environmentalism in British Columbia, "Misrepresented Redwashing", http://www.firstnations.de/indian_land/misrepresented-redwashing.htm

22 Taylor Lorenz, "She's the investor guru for online creators",

New York Times, 1 September 2021, https://www.nytimes.com/2021/09/01/technology/li-jin-youtube-creators.html

23　@SouthParkCommons, "Li Jin on The Passion Economy", YouTube, 2020, https://youtu.be/QbJv6kYejB4?t=2497

24　@katyperry, Instagram, 29 April 2022, https://www.instagram.com/p/Cc82MjOvDYV/?hl=fr

25　Nitasha Tiku, "Famous women join the crypto hustle, but it could cost their fans", *Washington Post*, 6 April 2022, https://www.washingtonpost.com/technology/2022/04/06/women-crypto-nft/

26　For more debunking of crypto and NFTs, go see @münecat's video on the topic, https://youtu.be/u-sNSjS8cq0 as well as @FoldingIdeas' video, https://youtu.be/YQ_xWvX1n9g

27　Sara Morrison, "Kim Kardashian's Instagram story just cost her $1.26 million", *Vox*, 3 October 2022, https://www.vox.com/recode/2022/10/3/23384955/kim-kardashian-crypto-ethereum-max-emax-sec

28　Hadrien Bureau, "Le macronisme, cette idéologie de l'individualisme béat et indigne qui ne dit pas son nom", *Huffington Post*, 4 March 2018, https://www.huffingtonpost.fr/politique/article/le-macronisme-cette-ideologie-de-l-individualisme-beat-et-indigne-qui-ne-dit-pas-son-nom_118924.html

29　The founder of Toyota was influenced by the book. Jeffrey K. Liker, *The Toyota Way*, New York: McGraw Hill, 2004, p. 17.

30　Socialist Robert Tressell said that "Self-help by Smiles [is] suitable for perusal by persons suffering from almost complete obliteration of the mental faculties", Robert Tressell, *The Ragged-Trousered Philanthropists*, London: Grant Richards Ltd, 1914, p. 289.

31　Nicolas Martin-Breteau, *Corps Politiques : Le sport dans les luttes des Noirs américains pour l'égalité depuis la fin du XIXème siècle*, Paris : Editions EHESS, 2020, p. 42.

32 Booker T. Washington, *Up From Slavery: An Autobiography*, New York: Doubleday, 1963, p. 174-175.

33 W.E.B. Du Bois, *The Philadelphia Negro: A Social Study*, 1899, https://archive.org/stream/ philadelphianegr001901mbp/philadelphianegr 001901mbp_djvu.txt

34 Plato, *Apology*, 29d-29e.

35 See dialogue between Socrates and Alcibiades in Plato, Alcibiades.

36 Jean-Claude Bourguignon, "Techniques de soi", Christine Delory-Momberger ed., *Vocabulaire des histoires de vie et de la recherche biographique*, Toulouse : Érès, 2019, p. 388-391.

37 Michel Foucault, *The Hermeneutics of the Subject: Lectures at the Collège de France*, 1981-82, New York: Palgrave Macmillan, 2005, p.10.

38 Ibid.

39 Michel Foucault, *Discipline and Punish: The Birth of the Prison*, New York: Pantheon Books, 1977.

40 Ibid.

41 Byung-Chul Han, *Psychopolitics: Neoliberalism and New Technologies of Power*, London, New York: Verso, 2017, p. 8-9.

42 Arabelle Sicardi, "Beauty is Broken", *Medium*, 10 December 2015, https://medium.com/matter/beauty-is-broken-62dfd2be69df

43 Another reference to Susan Faludi's intervention in *C-Span*, 2 October 1992, https://www.c-span.org/video/?33591-1/ backlash

Chapter 2: Traditional Femininity is Making a Comeback

1 @LeQuotidien, "Martin Weill face à Jordan B. Peterson", YouTube, 12 December 2018, https://www.youtube.com/ watch?v=CzZDed4gEHc

2 In France, the term "republican" refers to the national motto

"Liberté, Égalité, Fraternité" (Liberty, Equality, Fraternity), but in this context, it is politicised to refer to France's white, bourgeois, Judeo-Christian heritage.

3   "Tenue Républicaine pour aller à l'école: Jean-Michel Blanquer moqué sur Twitter", *Radio France*, 21 September 2020, https://www.radiofrance.fr/franceinter/tenue-republicaine-pour-aller-a-l-ecole-jean-michel-blanquer-moque-sur-twitter-8329567

4   @FreshandFit, "If She Uses THIS, She's 100% Cheating on You… (Accept It)", YouTube, 22 May 2021, https://www.youtube.com/watch?v=F0M2Bk_x_Dw

5   About Anna, AnnaBey.com, last consulted on 01/05/2023.

6   Sadie Nicholas on Tradwives, *Daily Mail*, 25 January 2020, https://www.dailymail.co.uk/femail/article-7926581/How-Tradwives-sacrifice-careers-satisfy-husbands-whim.html

7   @oliSUNvia, "stop denying women their autonomy", YouTube, November 2022, https://www.youtube.com/watch?v=asjmdBOUjQI

8   Michaele L. Ferguson, "Choice Feminism and the Fear of Politics", *Perspectives on Politics*, vol. 8, no.1, 2010, p. 247—53, JSTOR, http://www.jstor.org/stable/25698532.

9   Françoise Vergès, *A Decolonial Feminism*, London: Pluto Press, 2019, p.48.

10 Michaele L. Ferguson, "Choice Feminism and the Fear of Politics".

11 TikTok videos found in @HasanAbi's reaction video, "What Is "Trad-Wife" Tiktok???", YouTube, 6 September 2022, https://www.youtube.com/watch?v=jvynIx-8el0

12 G.K. Chesterton, "Social Reform versus Birth Control", 1927, http://www.gkc.org.uk/gkc/books/Social_Reform_B.C.html

13 Aaron Russo, L'interview en français (2007), YouTube, https://www.youtube.com/watch?v=owXtjrWACLg

14   Susan Faludi, *Backlash: The Undeclared War Against American Women*, New York: Three Rivers Press, 1993, p.82--83.

15   "Speech: Revolution: It's Not Easy, Quick, or Pretty", *The Black Agenda Review*, 29 June 2022, https://www.blackagendareport. com/speech-revolution-its-not-easy-quick-or-pretty-pat-parker-1980

16   Richard Reeves, *Of Boys and Men: Why the Modern Man is Struggling, Why it Matters, and What to Do about It*, Washington D.C.: Brookings Institution Press, 2022; Stephanie Durieu for Insee, "Les femmes sont plus scolarisées et diplômées que les hommes, mais davantage au chômage", 2015, https://www.insee.fr/fr/statistiques/1285500

17   "The Case Against the Sexual Revolution", Mikhaila Peterson's Podcast, Ep.165, October 2022.

18   "Cyrus North, Penseur et YouTubeur — Êtes-vous vraiment heureux ?", InPower by Louise Aubéry, November 2021.

19   Sadie Nicholas on Tradwives, *Daily Mail*, op cit. 1

20   @StrangeAeons, "Tradwives & The Tumblr #Girl Ecosystem", YouTube, August 2022, https://youtu.be/SXGBYAOMLsA

21   As found in Lauren Bastide, *Futur.es*, Paris: Allary, 2022, quoting François Kraus, "L'inégale répartition des tâches ménagères ou la persistance d'un privilège de genre", Fondation Jean Jaurès and IFOP, November 2019; Édouard Louis, A Woman's Battles and Transformations, New York : Farrar, Straus and Giroux, 2022.

22   @TeeNoir, "Masculinity, Submission, and a Black Woman's Place", YouTube, 30 June 2022, https://youtu.be/Sl5_u7kE7Ks

23   Miguel Dean, "Balancing the masculine and feminine within", migueldean.net.

24   Echols, *Daring to Be Bad,* p.5.

25   @Cass_Andre, "GUERRE des sexes au CHALET - Épisode 2 ft. Raz404", Twitch, https://www.twitch.tv/videos/1729439196?filter=all&sort=time

26   "Que sont devenus les tirailleurs après les guerres ? – CceSoir",
     YouTube, 4 January 2022, https://www.youtube.com/
     watch?v=qSuLShdJxXg

27   Melissa V. Harris, *Sister Citizen: Shame, Stereotypes, and Black Women
     in America*, New Haven: Yale University Press, 2011, p. 35-50.

28   Nicolas Martin-Breteau, *Corps Politiques: Le sport dans les luttes des
     Noirs américains pour l'égalité depuis la fin du XIXème siècle*, Paris :
     Éditions EHESS, 2020, p. 114-15.

29   Ibid, 115.

30   Ibid, 116-117.

31   @TeeNoir, "Masculinity, Submission, and a Black Woman's
     Place", YouTube.

32   Kimberly Jade Norwood, ""If You Is White, You's Alright. . . ."
     Stories About Colorism in America", *Washington University in St.
     Louis Law Review*, 2015.

33   See @FDSignifier, @TeeNoir, and @KhadijaMbowe YouTube
     videos on the topic.

34   Trina Jones, "Shades of Brown: The Law of Skin Color", 49
     Duke Law Journal, 2000.

35   Amanda Maryanna, "why can't black women be the love
     interest?", YouTube, 15 February 2021, https://youtu.be/
     HzBVpoVa26k

36   @FreshandFit, YouTube, https://www.youtube.com/@
     FreshFitMiami/featured

37   Wendy Wang, "Interracial marriage: Who is "marrying out"?",
     Pew Research Center, 12 June 2015.

38   Ibid.

39   Amia Srinivasan, *The Right to Sex: Feminism in the Twenty-First
     Century*, New York: Farrar, Straus and Giroux, 2021.

40   @BreenyLee, "Never EVER "Submit" To A Man (LIKE
     THIS)", YouTube, July 2022, https://youtu.be/Lg4TFc-ydaM

41   Ibid.

42   This is inspired by writer Leopold Ségar Senghor's work on

"Négritude" and "Métissage", see https://poets.org/text/brief-guide-negritude

43 @BBCStories, "Submitting to my husband like it's 1959", YouTube, January 2020, https://youtu.be/ZwT-zYo4-OM?

44 Ibid.

45 Ibid.

46 @TaraMooknee, "The "Stay-At-Home Girlfriend" TikTok trend: a case study in manufactured outrage", YouTube, 13 October 2022, https://www.youtube.com/watch?v=o1NbJgDqUyc

47 Ibid.

48 @NBCNews, "Kellyanne Conway Talks "Conservative Feminism" at CPAC", YouTube, February 2017, https://youtu.be/kPSuLXthgBc

49 Ibid.

50 Sara Hammel, "Sarah Palin's Close Encounter with a Real Mama Bear", *People*, 19 October 2010, https://people.com/pets/sarah-palins-close-encounter-with-a-real-mama-bear/

51 Linda K. Kerber, "The Republican Mother: Women and the Enlightenment — An American Perspective", in *Toward an Intellectual History of Women: Essays by Linda K. Kerber*, Chapel Hill: University of North Carolina Press, 1997, p. 43.

52 Grace Deason, "The psychology of maternal politics: priming and framing effects of candidates' appeals to motherhood, Politics, Groups, and Identities", *Politics, Groups, and Identities*, vol.2, no.2, 2020, p.90—101.

53 @MiaMulder, "Transinvestigation: The Conspiracy Theory That Everyone Is Transgender", YouTube, September 2022, https://youtu.be/QH5-MDXzfmg

54 @ARTE, "Toutes musclées", YouTube, October 2022, https://youtu.be/rdDJUn55Z3M

55 Ibid.

56 Florence Carpentier, "Alice Milliat: A Feminist Pioneer for

Women's Sport", in *Global Sport Leaders: A Biographical Analysis of International Sport Management*, London: Palgrave Macmillan, 2018, p. 61-81.

57 "In Amsterdam in 1928, Lina Radke was the first female Olympic 800m champion, but…", Official Olympics Website, https://olympics.com/en/news/in-amsterdam-in-1928-lina-radke-was-the-first-female-olympic-800m-champion-but

58 Ibid.

59 @WhitneySimmons, "FOLLOWING MY OLD UNHEALTHY FULL DAY OF EATING", November 2019, https://youtu.be/36nVW6D3dSE

60 @ARTE, "Toutes musclées"

61 @StephanieButtermore, "Honest Q&A w/ My Boyfriend: Weight Gain, "All In", Binge Eating, My Haters ft. Jeff Nippard", YouTube, October 2019, https://youtu.be/VXrhuGWONdY

62 @ARTE, "Toutes musclées"

63 Anaïs Bohuon, *Le Test de féminité dans les compétitions sportives. Une histoire classée X ?*, Paris : Éditions IXe, 2012.

64 @MiaMulder, "Transinvestigation: The Conspiracy Theory That Everyone Is Transgender", YouTube, September 2022, https://youtu.be/QH5-MDXzfmg

65 "Intersex people, OHCHR and the human rights of LGBTI people", United Nations Human Rights Office of the High Commissioner, https://www.ohchr.org/en/sexual-orientation-and-gender-identity/intersex-people

66 Abigail Thorn, "Have we got it wrong on dysphoria?", *Trans Writes*, 15 June 2022, https://transwrites.world/have-we-got-it-wrong-on-dysphoria-abigail-thorn-discusses-trans-healthcare/

67 @PhilosophyTube, "I Emailed My Doctor 133 Times: The Crisis In the British Healthcare System", YouTube, November 2022, https://youtu.be/v1eWIshUzr8

Part II: A Failed Sexual Revolution?

1   "Spain passes toughened 'Only yes means yes' rape law",
    Le Monde, 26 August 2022, https://www.lemonde.fr/en/
    international/article/2022/08/26/spain-passes-toughened-only-
    yes-means-yes-rape-law_5994803_4.html

2   Laura Bates, *Men Who Hate Women*, London: Simon & Schuster
    UK, 2021, p. 93.

3   @MatSchaffer, "Why You Should Set Boundaries with Men
    (and HOW to do it)", YouTube, 2019, https://youtu.be/
    oslEy98zMEQ

4   @StephanSpeaks, "A Lack of Boundaries Invites a Lack of
    Respect", YouTube, 2019, https://youtu.be/eW26DZgaNCg

5   Katherine Angel, *Tomorrow Sex Will Be Good Again: Women and
    Desire in the Age of Consent*, London: Verso, 2021, p. 9.

6   Alison Segel, "Why Women Should Always Make The First
    Move In Dating, According To Bumble's CEO", *Elite Daily*,
    April 2017, https://www.elitedaily.com/dating/women-bumble-
    dating/2003863

7   Amia Srinivasan, *The Right to Sex.*

8   Andrew Callaghan, accused of sexual misconduct and
    sexual assault, said he held that belief in a response video
    he published on his channel, https://www.youtube.com/
    watch?v=aQt3TgIo5e8

9   A question raised by Katherine Angel in *Tomorrow Sex Will Be
    Good Again.*

10 Andrew Callaghan's response video can be found on YouTube,
    https://www.youtube.com/watch?v=aQt3TgIo5e8

11 @_mia_india_, Instagram, 13 January 2023, https://www.
    instagram.com/p/CnWwpRtMfmx/

12 Eva Illouz, *The End of Love: A Sociology of Negative Relations*, Oxford:
    Oxford University Press, 2019.

13 Irving Howe, quoted by Judith Shulevitz in "Kate Millett:
    'Sexual Politics' Family Values," *The New York Review of Books*, 29
    September 2017.

14　I made an Instagram story with a screenshot of the interaction between V and Interviewer and asked my followers: "do you agree that this interaction is a normal Tinder interaction like V says it is?" Among the 923 replies I received, 822 voted "No" and 121 voted "Yes".

15　Illouz, *The End of Love*, p.63.

16　Jen Christensen, "Why men use masturbation to harass women", CNN, 11 November 2017, https://edition.cnn.com/2017/11/09/health/masturbation-sexual-harassment/index.html

17　@MaddieDragsbaek, "the hoe phase to celibacy pipeline", YouTube, December 2022, https://www.youtube.com/watch?v=2ih11okCTag

18　The study was conducted on Google Forms, in August 2022. I collected 450 answers. 62.2% of participants identified as female, 30.7% as men and 6.4% as non-binary. 50.4% identified as heterosexual, 31.7% as bisexual, 9.7% as pansexual, 6% as homosexual, 1.5% as asexual. 48.4% were between the ages of 18-25, 47.1% between 25-34 and 3.3% between the ages of 35-44.

19　Émile Durkheim, Suicide, p. 234; Émile Durkheim, Le suicide: Étude de sociologie, Paris: F. Alcan, 1897, p. 304–305.

20　Illouz, *The End of Love*, , p.89.

21　Ibid., 188.

22　Ibid., 82.

23　Philip Eil, "Here's Why it's Still Really Hard to Get Men to Go to Therapy", *Vice*, 22 November 2017, https://www.vice.com/en/article/43nzag/men-dont-go-therapy-mental-health

24　Melinda Cooper, *Family Values: Between Neoliberalism and the New Social Conservatism*, Cambridge: Zone / Near Futures, 2017, p.10.

25　Ibid., 14.

26 Ibid., 17.

27 Ibid., 18.

Chapter 1: The Will to Not Change

1   Jim Taylor, "The woman who founded the 'incel' movement", *BBC*, 30 August 2018, https://www.bbc.com/news/world-us-canada-45284455

2   Laura Bates quoting Dr Lisa Sugiura, Men Who Hate Women, 2020, p. 20-21.

3   Phrase coined by sociologist Sylvie Laurent to refer to the millions of pro-Trump White Americans who fear racial dispossession.

4   Sylvie Laurent, Pauvre petit Blanc : Le mythe de la dépossession raciale, Paris : Maison des Sciences de l'Homme, 2020.

5   @PiersMorganUncensored, "Jordan Peterson Gets Emotional Talking About Olivia Wilde's 'Incel' Comparison", YouTube, September 2022, https://youtu.be/M1612L2FMHo

6   Bates, *Men Who Hate Women*, 2021, p. 35.

7   Angel, *Tomorrow Sex Will Be Good Again*, p. 67.

8   https://looksmaxxing.com

9   Srinivasan, *The Right to Sex*, p.119.

10 Anthony Robbins, *Awaken the Giant Within: How to Take Immediate Control of Your Mental, Emotional, Physical and Financial Life*, New York: Downtown Press, 2001, Chapter 2.

11 @Jubilee, "Men's Rights vs Feminism: Is Toxic Masculinity Real? | Middle Ground", YouTube, December 2019, https://youtu.be/hOUGNGWmN0k

12 @Popculturedetective, "Born Sexy Yesterday", YouTube, April 2017, https://youtu.be/0thpEyEwi80

13 @TheSchoolofLife, "Why Nice People Are Scary", YouTube, 31 August 2015, https://www.youtube.com/watch?v=IBsOu44Tj2E

14 @zackbarbour, "Reasons why I'd make a bad boyfriend..",

TikTok, https://www.tiktok.com/@zackbarbour/
video/7137011763052072238?q=zack%20barbour%20
reasons%20why&t=1683532396625

15 @MotivationMadnessChannel, "Jordan Peterson: Why Do Nice
Guys Always Finish Last", YouTube, March 2018, https://youtu.
be/di2FM8WZI5E

16 @MikhailaPeterson, "Wokeism, Advice to Teens and the Dangers
of Casual Relationships / Jordan Peterson", YouTube, June 2022,
https://youtu.be/YaZOvH5dXDI

17 "Charisma University", https://www.charismaoncommand.
com/coc-charisma-university/

18 @TheTake, "The Nice Guy Trope, Explained",
YouTube, 22 February 2020, https://www.youtube.com/
watch?v=8JkZ55np3z8

19 Taylor Tomlinson, *Quarter-Life Crisis*, Directed by Marcus Raboy,
2020.

20 @YesVousAime, "La drague féministe : prenons des notes ! -
Broute - CANAL+", YouTube, 21 March 2021, https://www.
youtube.com/watch?v=g-AAr5Mqi1s

21 @Kidology, "Men reject women too. That's why I'm celibate.",
YouTube, 21 October 2022, https://www.youtube.com/
watch?v=t2T3hv0ZMZI

22 Reeves, *Of Boys and Men*, p.107.

23 Messner, Michael A. Messner, "Essentialist retreat: the
mythopoetic men's movement and the Christian promise
keepers", *Politics of Masculinities: Men in Movements*. Lanham:
AltaMira Press, 2000, p. 17.

24 Ibid., pp. 17-23.

25 @PatrickCc:, "The Dark Reality of Andrew Tate's Rose
To Fame…", YouTube, 16 August 2022, https://youtu.be/
HJ4xoxYAya4

26 Daniel Geary, "The Moynihan Report: An Annotated
Version", *The Atlantic*, https://www.theatlantic.com/politics/

archive/2015/09/the-moynihan-report-an-annotated-edition/404632/

27 Ibid.

28 "Jordan Peterson — Don't Be The Nice Guy", lecture found on the Clash of Ideas channel, YouTube, https://youtu.be/fesSvXKxYd0

29 Ed West, "How single men and women are making politics more extreme", *The Week*, 4 August 2017, https://theweek.com/articles/715794/how-single-men-women-are-making-politics-more-extreme

30 @CrowderBits, "Billie Eilish Doesn't Understand Empowerment | Louder With Crowder", YouTube, May 2021, https://youtu.be/LG4FUTrGEkI

31 "What is MKP?", mankindproject.org

32 "L'identité masculine en question | ARTE Regards", *Arte.tv*, January 2023, https://www.arte.tv/fr/videos/106725-005-A/arte-regards-l-identite-masculine-en-questions/

33 Jean-Loup Adenor, "Qu'est-ce que le 'Mankind Project', ce groupe masculiniste soupçonné de dérives sectaires?", *Marianne*, 7 November 2022, https://www.marianne.net/societe/laicite-et-religions/quest-ce-que-le-mankind-project-ce-groupe-masculiniste-soupconne-de-derives-sectaires

34 Léane Alestra and Vinciane Despret, "C'est dans la nature, le mâle est dominant", *Mescréantes Podcast*, April 2020.

35 Elise Kjørstad, "Wolf packs don't actually have alpha males and alpha females, the idea is based on a misunderstanding", *Science Norway*, 26 April 2021, https://sciencenorway.no/ulv/wolf-packs-dont-actually-have-alpha-males-and-alpha-females-the-idea-is-based-on-a-misunderstanding/1850514

36 Ibid.

37 Jean-Claude Dreher, et al., "Testosterone causes both prosocial and antisocial status-enhancing behaviors in human males", *PNAS*, vol.113, no.41, September 2016, p.11633—11638.

38 Michelle Goldberg, "The Shame of the MeToo Men", New York Times, 14 September 2018, https://www.nytimes.com/2018/09/14/opinion/columnists/metoo-movement-franken-hockenberry-macdonald.html

39 Srinivasan, *The Right To Sex*, p.20.

40 Laure Bretton, "'D'homme à homme' : la double offense de Macron", *Libération*, 15 July 2020, https://www.liberation.fr/politiques/2020/07/15/d-homme-a-homme-la-double-offense-de-macron_1794289/

41 "Sur TF1 et LCI, Emmanuel Macron défend le maintien au gouvernement de Nicolas Hulot accusé de viol", *TF1 Info*, 15 December 2021, https://www.tf1info.fr/politique/sur-tf1-et-lci-emmanuel-macron-defend-le-maintien-au-gouvernement-de-nicolas-hulot-accuse-de-viol-2204710.html

42 Andrew Smiler, *Is Masculinity Toxic?: A Primer for the 21st Century*, London: Thames and Hudson Ltd, 2019, p.124.

43 Bastide, *Futur.es*, p.144.

44 @IntelligenceSquared, Jordan Peterson on Gender, Patriarchy and the Slide Towards Tyranny, YouTube, May 2018, https://youtu.be/7QRQjrsFnR4

45 Megan Brenan, "Americans No Longer Prefer Male Boss to Female Boss", *News Gallup*, 16 November 2017, https://news.gallup.com/poll/222425/americans-no-longer-prefer-male-boss-female-boss.aspx

46 Racha Belmehdi, *Rivalité, nom féminin : Une lecture féministe du mythe*, Lausanne : Favre, 2022.

47 Bates, *Men Who Hate Women*, p. 35-40.

48 @LittleJoel, "Men and the Left", YouTube, 2 January 2023, https://youtu.be/R0_1a2cGFDw

49 As quoted in Jane Ward, *The Tragedy of Heterosexuality*, New York: New York University Press, 2020. p.12.

50 @TaraMooknee "Heterofatalism: WHY straight women aren't okay.", YouTube, July 2021, https://www.youtube.com/watch?v=S4xCbmCG2Rc

51 Asa Seresin, "On Heteropessimism", *The New Inquiry*, 9 October 2019, https://thenewinquiry.com/on-heteropessimism/

52 Ibid.

53 Ward, *The Tragedy of Heterosexuality*, p.9.

54 Chantal Jaquet, *Les Transclasses ou la non-reproduction*, Paris: PUF, 2014.

55 If you want to dig a bit more into the surveillance aspect of TV reality shows, I recommend you watch @BroeyDeschanel's video "Love Island: A Flirtation With Surveillance", YouTube, 29 September 2021, https://www.youtube.com/watch?v=S8VqPxYM2tY&

56 Participants were asked to share a positive experience with a dating app. I collected 453 answers (62.3% female, 30.7% male, 7% non-binary; 48.3% between the age of 18-24, 47.2% between the age of 25-34, 4.5% 35+)

57 @VersoBooks, "Abolish the family. Sophie Lewis speaks to Ben Smoke", YouTube, October 2022, https://youtu.be/5FiD2JGrM3s

58 @CCeSoir, "L'inflation va-t-elle durer ? ", YouTube, 9 November 2022, https://www.youtube.com/watch?v=QHnAmgIdqCw

59 @Blast, "L'amour: une arme révolutionnaire", YouTube, 24 August 2022, https://youtu.be/F45K7ssH3fs

60 Found in Bastide, *Futur.es*, 2022, quoting François Kraus, "L'inégale répartition des tâches ménagères ou la persistance d'un privilège de genre", *Fondation Jean Jaurès*, November 2019, https://www.jean-jaures.org/publication/linegale-repartition-des-taches-menageres-ou-la-persistance-dun-privilege-de-genre/

61 Isabel Slone, "Escape Into Cottagecore, Calming Ethos for Our Febrile Moment", *New York Times*, 10 March 2020, https://www.nytimes.com/2020/03/10/style/cottagecore.html

62 James Simpson, "More than an Aesthetic — Cottagecore and Queerness", *Redbrick*, 23 August 2022, https://www.redbrick.me/more-than-an-aesthetic-cottagecore-and-queerness/

63 @HitomiMochizuki, "Sacred Sisterhood | making friends when you have trauma and social anxiety *healing*", YouTube, 2021, https://youtu.be/dN3TtkMI0Po

64 Fabienne Brugère, *L'éthique du « care »*, Paris: PUF, 2011. p.11.

65 Ibid., 20.

66 Evelyne Pieiller, "La tyrannie de la bienveillance", *Le Monde Diplomatique*, December 2020, p.3, https://www.monde-diplomatique.fr/2020/12/PIEILLER/62545

67 Angélique Del Rey, "Attention au 'care' …" *Le Monde Diplomatique*, January 2013, https://www.monde-diplomatique.fr/2013/01/DEL_REY/48621

68 Emma Taggart, "7 Women Built Their Dream Retirement Home to Live Their Last Days Together", *My Modern Met*, 10 July 2019, https://mymodernmet.com/dream-retirement-home-friends/

69 Anna North, "Older Ladies Living Together Is An Awesome Trend", Jezebel, 17 November 2011, https://jezebel.com/older-ladies-living-together-is-an-awesome-trend-5860636; Sarah Mahoney, "The New Housemates", *AARP The Magazine*, July 2007, https://www.aarp.org/home-garden/housing/info-2007/the_new_housemates.html

70 Anna Boyles, "Boston marriages and the queer history of women's suffrage", City of Boston's Official Website, https://www.boston.gov/news/boston-marriages-and-queer-history-womens-suffrage#:~:text=The%20term%20"Boston%20Marriage"%20refers,middle%20or%20upper%2Dclass%20women.

71 Yuhe Faye Wang, "Heterosexuality and its discontents",

Outline, 28 January 2020, https://theoutline.com/post/8607/heteropessimism-why-women-date-men

72 Emily Baldoni, "The Invisible Work of Women", *The Man Enough Podcast*, August 2021.

73 Luc Boltanski, Éve Chiapello, *Le Nouvel Esprit du Capitalisme*, Paris : Gallimard, 1999.

74 @Blast, "L'amour: une arme révolutionnaire", YouTube, 24 August 2022, https://youtu.be/F45K7ssH3fs

75 Costanza Spina, "Censored n°4 'Chrysalide'", September 2020, https://manifesto-21.com/nous-sommes-a-laube-dune-revolution-romantique-intersectionnelle/

76 @Blast, "L'amour: une arme révolutionnaire", YouTube.

77 @ProgressiveInternational, "Red Valentine's: Love & Revolution", YouTube, 14 February 2021, https://www.youtube.com/live/LtWq26Ag7DI?feature=share

78 Echols, *Daring to Be Bad*, p.61.

79 Elaine Brown, *A Taste of Power: A Black Woman's Story*, New York: Anchor, 1993.

80 @ItsComplicatedChannel, "POWER OF THE P*SSY & BEING HONEST: Rules of Modern Dating & Understanding Women" YouTube, November 2021, https://www.youtube.com/watch?v=2ELtpqAK99o

81 @KhadijaMbowe, "Issa scam? Desirability unpacked… | Khadija Mbowe", YouTube, February 2023, https://www.youtube.com/watch?v=lnxQeh7Rsog

82 @TeeNoir "Hypersexuality & the Perfect P*ssy Complex", YouTube, September 2022, https://www.youtube.com/watch?v=U9QzbV4D8VQ

83 Anthropologist Oscar Lewis wrote in 1969 an article titled "The Culture of Poverty" in which he theorised that a culture of poverty was transmitted from one generation to the next.

The article was a source of inspiration for other scholars and journalists. Many sociologists, including Massey and Denton, used the concept of the "underclass" in their work until the term became too controversial. See Herbert Gans, "From 'Underclass' to 'Undercase': Some Observations About the Future of the Post-Industrial Economy and its Major Victims" in *Urban Poverty and the Underclass* (edited by Enzo Mingione), Cambridge: Blackwell Publishers, 1996, pp. 141–152, for a thorough criticism of the concept of the "underclass".

84   Ibid.

85   Micheal Arceneaux, "Op-Ed: Um, So Here's The Problem With That Nicki Minaj Interview", *Essence*, updated on 23 October 2020, https://www.essence.com/celebrity/op-ed-did-nicki-minaj-elle-magazine-interview-mixed-messages/

86   On 9 June 2019.

87   Gigi Fong, "Sex Work and Fashion Are More Closely Related Than You Think", *Yahoo!*, 7 April 2022.

88   @KhadijaMbowe, "Are we turning away from Seggs Positive Feminism?", YouTube, August 2022, https://youtu.be/Idmegxtis8I

89   @KhadijaMbowe, "Issa scam? Desirability unpacked…"

90   @Djvlad, "Cardi B : I Became a Stripper to Escape Domestic Violence", YouTube, January 2016, https://youtu.be/vzfcNl-o9bI

91   @SimonPuech, "Ces étudiantes se prostituent (Enquête)", YouTube, January 2022, https://youtu.be/Ua8qK-QZiWg

92   Claire Reid, "51-Year-Old Millionaire Who Said 'Love Was For Poor People' Set To Marry 21-Year-Old Girlfriend", *LADBible*, March 2022, https://www.ladbible.com/news/millionaire-51-set-to-marry-girlfriend-21-20220310

93   @HasanAbi, "The Amouranth Situation…", YouTube, 17 October 2022, https://www.youtube.com/watch?v=oQEKsfXg_bY

94 @PatrickCc:, "The Dark Reality of Andrew Tate's Rose To Fame...", YouTube.

95 Emily Ratajkowski, "Buying Myself Back: When does a model own her own image?", *The Cut*, 15 September 2020, https://www.thecut.com/article/emily-ratajkowski-owning-my-image-essay.html

96 Ibid.

97 "Of Money and Men: Emily Ratajkowski in Conversation with Amia Srinivasan", *Interview Magazine*, 16 November 2021, https://www.interviewmagazine.com/culture/of-money-and-men-emily-ratajkowski-in-conversation-with-amia-srinivasan

98 Asks @TeeNoir in "Is it REALLY possible to 'Sleep Your Way to the Top'?", YouTube, October 2021, https://youtu.be/6mdKdhAG2ZU

Chapter 2: Making Society Pure Again

1 Kelsey Weekman, "What happens to Christian influencers when they get married?", *BuzzFeed News*, 6 July 2022, https://www.buzzfeednews.com/article/kelseyweekman/christian-influencers-purity-culture-marriage

2 @Jouelzy, "Casual Sex Sucks", YouTube, February 2022, https://youtu.be/4i65JDqnR3g

3 Alice Schlegel, "Status, Property, and the Value on Virginity", *American Ethnologist*, vol.18, no.4, p.724.

4 @IntelexualMedia, "A Short History of Virginity", YouTube, 10 March 2021, https://youtu.be/XX4pPg2DO5E

5 "A Visit With Aretha Franklin", *Jet Mag*, 2 May 1974.

6 @IntelexualMedia, "A Short History of Virginity", YouTube.

7 Amnesty International report on Women, Violence, and Health, August 2021.

8 Lee Moran, *Daily Mail*, November 2013, https://www.dailymail.co.uk/news/article-2510425/Brazilian-student-auctioned-virginity-hopes-sell-AGAIN.html

9   David Moye, *Huffington Post*, April 2014, https://www.huffpost. com/entry/elizabeth-raine-virginity-auction_n_5002502

10 Siofra Brennan, *Daily Mail*, December 2018, https://www. dailymail.co.uk/femail/article-6467261/British-student-18- reveals-shes-selling-virginity-online.html

11 Patrick Wintour, "Mahsa Amini Protests: The Big Story", *The Guardian Weekly*, 14 October 2022.

12 @IntelexualMedia, "A Short History of Virginity", YouTube.

13 @HasanAbi, "Steven Crowder LOSES HIS MIND Over Billie Eilish Photoshoot", YouTube, May 2021, https://youtu.be/ XmpQ4mdp45Y

14 De Elizabeth, "Billie Eilish Reveals the Reason for Her Baggy Clothes in New Calvin Klein Ad", *Teen Vogue*, 11 May 2019, https://www.teenvogue.com/story/billie-eilish-baggy-clothes- calvin-klein

15 Samantha Cole, "'You Feel So Violated': Streamer QTCinderella Is Speaking Out Against Deepfake Porn Harassment", 13 February 2023, https://qoshe.com/vice/samantha-cole/-you- feel-so-violated-streamer-qtcinderella-is-speaking-out-against- deepfake-porn-harassment/155305584

16 Naomi Wolf, "Veiled Sexuality", *Project Syndicate*, 30 August 2008, https://www.project-syndicate.org/commentary/veiled- sexuality-2008-08

17 Ibid.

18 Ibid.

19 The title of this section is inspired by @F.D.Signifier's video on the topic, https://youtu.be/DEeCVdbQC6c

20 Eva Illouz (dir.), *Les marchandises émotionnelles. L'authenticité au temps du capitalisme*, Paris: Premier Parallèle, 2019.

21 @ProgressiveInternational, "Red Valentine's: Love & Revolution", YouTube.

22 Ibid.

23 Leslie Green, "Pornographies", *Journal of Political Philosophy*, vol.27, no.8, 2000, p.27-52.

24 Kelsey Weekman, "What happens to Christian influencers when they get married?", *BuzzFeed News*

25 @PatrickCc:, "The Dark Reality of Andrew Tate's Rose To Fame...", YouTube.

26 As found in Noah Samsen's, "This Podcast Hates Women", YouTube, 14 April 2022, https://www.youtube.com/watch?v=CuZuaQ3a6SY

27 @FreshandFit, "WHY So MANY Women are Single Ft. RolloTomassi", YouTube, December 2021, https://www.youtube.com/watch?v=Si-oP7urIls

28 Lisa Portolan, "The Right Stuff: the new conservative dating app which has unsurprisingly, failed to attract women", *The Conversation*, 13 October 2022, https://theconversation.com/the-right-stuff-the-new-conservative-dating-app-which-has-unsurprisingly-failed-to-attract-women-192012

29 @Jouelzy, "Casual Sex Sucks", YouTube, February 2022, https://youtu.be/4i65JDqnR3g

30 Alice Cappelle, "Une Médecine d'Autodéfense ? Les Free Health Clinics du Black Panther Party", Master's Thesis, University of Lille, June 2021; Alondra Nelson, *Body and Soul: The Black Panther Party and The Fight Against Medical Discrimination*, Minneapolis: University of Minnesota Press, 2011.

31 Molly M. Ginty, "Our Bodies, Ourselves Turns 35 Today", Women's eNews, https://womensenews.org/2004/05/our-bodies-ourselves-turns-35-today/

32 @MikhailaPeterson, "The Case Against the Sexual Revolution", YouTube, October 2022, https://youtu.be/5JbDbt4dk3M

33 Ibid.

34 Rachel Cooke, "*The Case Against the Sexual Revolution* by Louise Perry review – a potent, plain-speaking womanifesto", *Guardian*, 6

June 2022, https://www.theguardian.com/books/2022/jun/06/
the-case-against-the-sexual-revolution-by-louise-perry-review-an-
act-of-insurrection-a-new-guide-to-sex-in-the-21st-century

35 @SpectatorTV, Fraser Nelson interviewed Louise Perry, "Louise
Perry: The feminist case for marriage", YouTube, 8 June 2022,
https://youtu.be/tQmzEAR-psc

36 Office for National Statistics, Divorces in England and Wales:
2015, 1950 to 2015 (2017).

37 @MikhailaPeterson, "The Case Against the Sexual Revolution",
YouTube.

38 Jenni Reid, "Russia is offering a hero's medal and $16,000 to
women who have ten kids", *CNBC*, 18 August 2022, https://
www.cnbc.com/2022/08/18/russia-offers-mother-heroine-
medal-and-16800-for-having-10-children.html

39 John Timsit, "Éric Zemmour propose une bourse de 10.000
euros pour toute nouvelle naissance dans la France rurale",
Figaro, 28 January 2022, https://www.lefigaro.fr/politique/
eric-zemmour-propose-une-bourse-de-10-000-euros-pour-toute-
nouvelle-naissance-dans-la-france-rurale-20220128

40 Clément Guillou, "Marine Le Pen profite du débat sur les
retraites pour défendre sa politique nataliste", *Le Monde*,
3 February 2023, https://www.lemonde.fr/politique/
article/2023/02/03/marine-le-pen-profite-du-debat-sur-les-
retraites-pour-defendre-sa-politique-nataliste_6160392_823448.
html#:~:text=En%202021%2C%20il%20avait%20
revu,PIB%20à%20la%20même%20échéance.

41 @MikhailaPeterson, "The Case Against the Sexual Revolution",
YouTube.

42 Melinda Cooper and Ben Mabie, "Family matters",
Viewpoint Magazine, 19 March 2018, https://viewpointmag.
com/2018/03/19/family-matters/

43 Ibid.

44 Andrew Wilson, "The Sexual Revolution Has Failed Women",
    The Gospel Coalition, 21 September 2022, https://www.
    thegospelcoalition.org/reviews/case-against-sexual-revolution-
    perry/

45 Alison Jasper, "Feminism and Religion" in Sarah Gamble (ed.),
    The Routledge Companion to Feminism and Postfeminism, London:
    Routledge, 2001.

46 Pierre Ancet, "Identité et sexualité chez Michel Foucault", in
    Daniel Welzer-Lang et al., *Masculinités : état des lieux*, Toulouse :
    Érès, 2011, p. 94 ; Michel Foucault, *The History of Sexuality*, New
    York: Pantheon Books, 1976.

Conclusion

1 David Graeber in "Bullshit jobs and the yoke of managerial
   feudalism" by N.B, *Economist*, 29 June 2018, https://www.
   economist.com/open-future/2018/06/29/bullshit-jobs-and-the-
   yoke-of-managerial-feudalism

2 Michele Barrett and Mary McIntosh, *The Anti-Social Family*, Nlb,
   1982, found in @Andrewism video titled 'Rethinking the Family',
   YouTube, 8 December 2021, https://www.youtube.com/
   watch?v=hmqNSCe0w2w

3 Tal Modesta, *Désirer à tout prix*, Paris: Binge Audio, 2022 ;
   Geoffroy de Lagasnerie, *3: Une aspiration du dehors*, Paris:
   Flammarion, 2023.

4 Ibid.

5 Self-defined progressive Philadelphia Congressional Candidate
   Alexandra Hunt declared on her Twitter feed that "we should
   be moving toward a right to sex. People should be able to have
   sex when they feel they want to, and we need to develop services
   that meet people's needs.' She used a study conducted by General

Social Survey dating from 2019 which shows that 28% men reported no sex in the past year (compared to 18% women).

6   Cf Louise Perry, *The Case Against the Sexual Revolution*.

7   @Straszfilms, "Identity, Gender, and VRChat (Why is everyone in VR an anime girl?)", YouTube, February 2021, https://youtu.be/5v_Dl7i4Bcw

8   Ibid.

9   Pawel Tacikowski et al., "Fluidity of gender identity induced by illusory body-sex change", *Scientific Reports* 10, 14385, 1 September 2020.

10   Legacy Russel, *Glitch Feminism*, London, New York: Verso, 2020.

11   Erik Olin Wright, *How to Be an Anti-Capitalist in the 21st Century*, London, New York: Verso, 2019, p.91.

12   Tarnoff, *Internet for the People*, p. 38.

13   Eric Hunting, "Solarpunk: Post-Industrial Design and Aesthetics", *Medium*, 18 July 2020, https://medium.com/@erichunting/solarpunk-post-industrial-design-and-aesthetics-1ecb350c28b6

Acknowledgments

As I regularly say in my videos, I am extremely lucky to be surrounded by incredibly smart, passionate, thoughtful and curious people that challenge me and encourage me to constantly consider new ways of thinking. This book is the product of all the deep conversations I've had with you at protests, in bars, buses, public toilets and whatnot.

I would like to start by saying a very special thanks to my sister (I honestly do not understand how she still wants to see me) who I have annoyed with this book more than anyone else. Constantly asking her what she thought about this or that argument I made, abruptly cutting conversations we were having to rush to my room and write down what just came to my mind. I would also like to say a special thanks to my dear friend François, the big brain energy meme in real life, who has accompanied my intellectual journey since undergrad and has since then recommended me an average of two books and three articles per day ☺. Thank you as well to my dearest friends Caroline, Marie and Sarah, whose intellect and emotional support has been a source of inspiration and strength for me. Thank you as well to Zo, a feminist rockstar who has inspired me to be more unapologetic, thank you to Augustin for radicalising me, thank you to Gwendoline, Nat, Luke, Célia and all the people mentioned above for advising me on my writing and helping me sharpen my arguments.

Thank you to Repeater Books for offering me the opportunity to write this book with a lot of freedom and ambition. Thank you in particular to Carl Neville and Tariq Godard for spotting me on the internet, specifically Tariq for your input, flexibility and for your trust. Thank you also to Christiana Spens, Josh Turner and Rhian E. Jones.

I cannot end this book without thanking my "colleagues", the content creators, video essayists and social commentators who have taught me so much in the past few years. I tried my best to convey in this book the value of their work, and how well they complement academia. I will certainly forget some people, but I recommend you check the work of (in no particular order) Tara Mooknee, Khadija Mbowe, Shanspeare, Film Fatales, Amanda Maryanna, Jouelzy, F.D Signifier, Madisyn Brown, Tee Noir, Noah Samsen, OliSUNvia, Tom Nicholas, Mina Le, Münecat, Folding Ideas, Big Joel, HBomberGuy, Philosophy Tube, Contrapoints, Jordan Theresa, Foreign Man in a Foreign Land, Broey Deschanel, Jessie Gender, Mia Mulder, TiffanyFerg, Adam Conover, Friendly Space Ninja, Kristen Leo, Princess Weekes, Kuncan Dastner, Intelexual Media, Lindsay Ellis, Adam Something, Jonas Čeika and Pop Culture Detective.

Finally thank you to my parents who have always supported me in my life choices and gave me a lot of freedom. Thank you to my mum for encouraging me to be curious and creative from a very early age and for her feminist values. Your strength through hardships will always be a source of inspiration for me. Thank you to my dad for his genuine positivity and for all the heated political debates we have had. I know I'll never convince you, but I'll keep trying.

REPEATER BOOKS

is dedicated to the creation of a new reality. The landscape of twenty-first-century arts and letters is faded and inert, riven by fashionable cynicism, egotistical self-reference and a nostalgia for the recent past. Repeater intends to add its voice to those movements that wish to enter history and assert control over its currents, gathering together scattered and isolated voices with those who have already called for an escape from Capitalist Realism. Our desire is to publish in every sphere and genre, combining vigorous dissent and a pragmatic willingness to succeed where messianic abstraction and quiescent co-option have stalled: abstention is not an option: we are alive and we don't agree.